The SOUTHWESTERN COMPANION

The SOUTHWESTERN COMPANION

Norman Kolpas

MALLARD PRESS
An imprint of
BDD Promotional Book Company, Inc.
666 Fifth Avenue
New York, New York 10103

A TERN ENTERPRISE BOOK

Published by MALLARD PRESS
An imprint of BDD Promotional Book Company, Inc.
666 Fifth Avenue
New York, New York 10103

Mallard Press and its accompanying design and logo are trademarks of BDD Promotional Book Company, Inc.

Copyright © 1991 by Michael Friedman Publishing Group, Inc.

First published in the United States of America in 1991 by Mallard Press.

ISBN 0-7924-5312-3

THE SOUTHWESTERN COMPANION
was prepared and produced by
Tern Enterprise, Inc.
15 West 26th Street
New York, New York 10010

Designer: Judy Morgan
Layout: Helayne Messing
Photography Editor: Ede Rothaus
Illustrations by: Judy L. Morgan

Additional Photography:

p. 33 © Joseph Saitta/courtesy of The Native American Art Gallery; p. 45, 53 © Guy Powers/Envision; p. 54, 91 © Lois Ellen Frank; p. 96–97 Lion by David Alvarez, photography © Lois Ellen Frank, from the collection of Norman Kolpas; p. 92 carved by Jimmy Koontz, photograph © Richard Todd, courtesy of the Alan and Cindy Horn Collection; p. 100 © Robert Reck; p. 104–105 © Bruce Burr/courtesy of The Native American Art Gallery

The recipe for Kachina Mosaic of Caviars with Endive Feathers, on page 61 is reprinted from *Modern Southwest Cuisine,* © 1986 by John Sedlar. Reprinted with permission of Simon & Schuster, Inc.; Grilled Baja Cabrilla with Bay Scallop Salsa, on page 62 is reprinted from *Janos: Recipes and Tales from a Southwest Restaurant,* © 1989 by Janos Wilder, with permission from Ten Speed Press, Berkeley, CA; Tamale Tart with Roast Garlic Custard and Gulf Coast Crabmeat on page 65 is courtesy of Steven Pyles, and is used with his permission; Green Chile and Oyster Chowder, on page 66 is reprinted from *Coyote Cafe,* © 1989 by Mark Miller, with permission from Ten Speed Press, Berkeley, CA.

Typeset by The Interface Group
Color Separations by Scantrans Pte. Ltd.
Printed and bound in Singapore by Tien Wah Press Pte. Ltd.

Dedication

For Jacob—who made his first visit to the Southwest at the age of three months and took it all in with wide-eyed awe—in the confident hope that his love of and respect for the region will continue to grow as he grows. And for Katie, who makes every journey and every project an adventure.

Acknowledgments

Many people, from those I spent hours talking with to others with whom I shared just a few brief words, contributed greatly to the information and impressions presented in this book. Those deserving particular thanks are Lois Ellen Frank, Philip Garaway, Steve Garcia, Ann Katzen, Jim and Kathy Katzen, Mark Miller, Stephen Pyles, John Sedlar, and Janos Wilder.

My wife, Katie, and our son, Jacob, were as always patient and enthusiastic throughout the laborious process of research and writing. Their contribution to this book is inestimable.

And special thanks are due to Stephen Williams, a good-humored, sensitive, and supportive editor, who from the beginning shared with me his own deep love of the Southwest. His enthusiasm for the region finds its way into these pages, too.

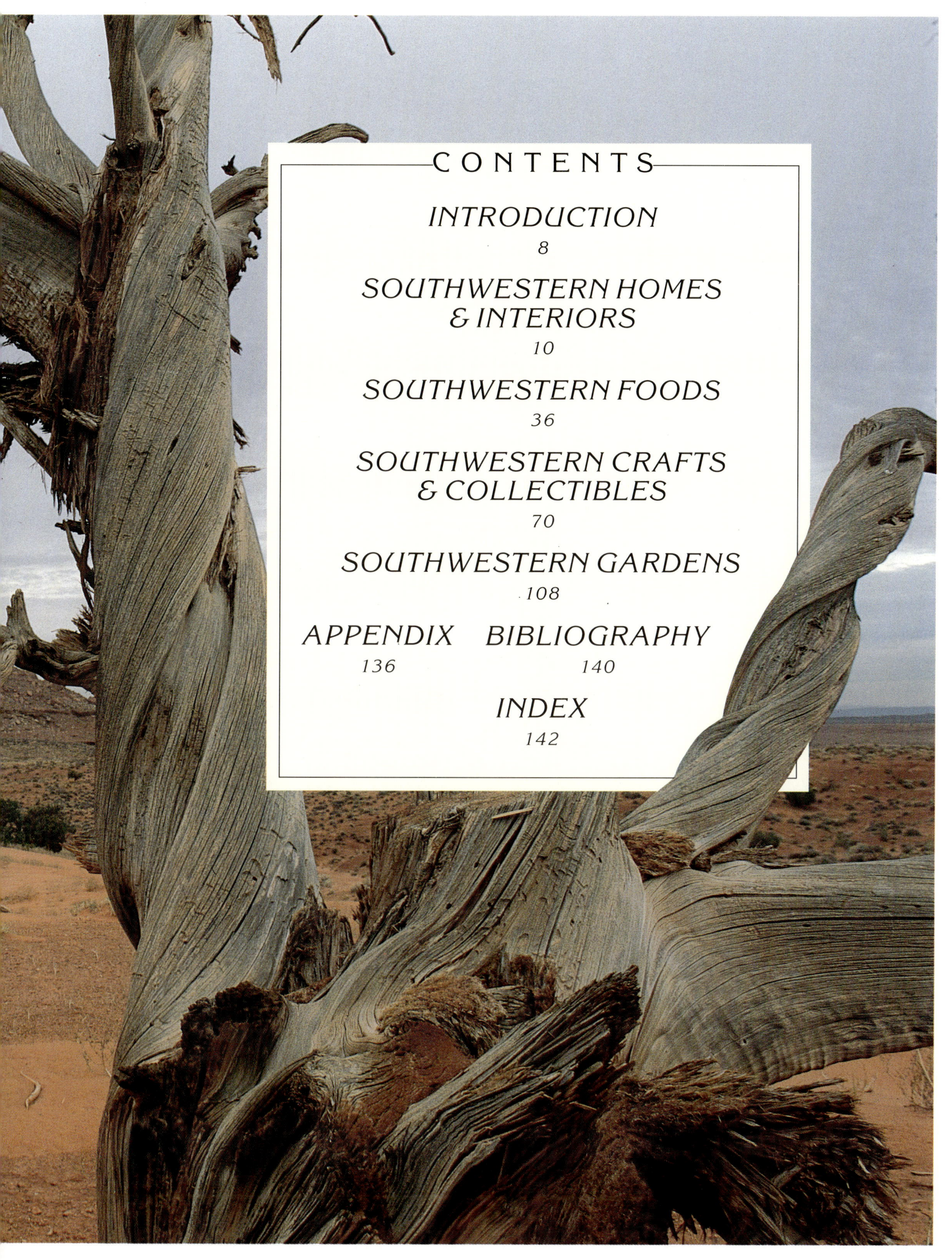

CONTENTS

What is *it about the Southwest?*

"The world is very wide here," the painter Georgia O'Keeffe observed, "and it's very hard to feel that it's wide in the East." The Southwest may well be largely desert, but it's a vast desert of uncommon beauty—from the red-bluff badlands of O'Keeffe's beloved northern New Mexico to the monolithic arches, mesas, and canyons of southern Utah, the sweeping panoramas of Arizona's Sonora desert valley to the breathtaking cliffsides of Colorado's Mesa Verde.

And it's a particularly hospitable desert, shot through by rivers and drenched by sudden storms. Native Americans have lived here for well more than nine thousand years. In the parched land, they learned to nurture plants that would provide them with their sustenance, including the corn, beans, and chiles that are the very basics of the Southwestern cooking we all know today. They built secure dwellings high on cliffsides throughout the region, fashioned from the same straw-flecked mud—adobe—that came to be the definitive building block of the Southwestern home.

Perhaps flecks of straw glinting in the sunlight on adobe walls gave rise to the legends of golden cities that initially lured Spanish explorers into the region. Spanish missionaries and settlers followed, infusing the Southwest with a rich Hispanic culture that,

despite numerous conflicts and uprisings, thrives today side by side with the Native American cultures. The early nineteenth century saw the first visits by Anglos from the East—American trappers, hunters, and traders—and the growing American presence in the region eventually led to war with Mexico and the ceding of Arizona and New Mexico to the United States in 1848.

And yet, thanks to geography and to the tenacity of Native American and Hispanic cultures, the Southwest remains a world resolutely apart from the rest of the nation, with a spirit completely its own. Traveling through the Southwest is like visiting another country without ever leaving home.

In the pages that follow, I try to explore both the strange and the familiar aspects of Southwestern culture and style, to provide a sampler by which you can begin your own explorations of this intriguing region. Perhaps, as was O'Keeffe on her first visit to Santa Fe, in the summer of 1917, you'll be hooked by your first experience of the Southwest. "I loved it immediately," she said. "From then on I was always on my way back."

—*Norman Kolpas*

SOUTHWESTERN HOMES & INTERIORS

The Native American peoples of the Southwest saw themselves as living in nature, at one with the forces that controlled the darkness and the light, the animals and the plants, the rain and the lightning. Their dwellings evolved out of that sense of oneness with the world around them, a meaning conveyed—without need of words—by one glimpse of the mountainous adobe high-rise of Taos Pueblo or the pre-Columbian cliff dwellings growing out of the rocky cliff faces at Mesa Verde.

With the Europeans came new concepts of the home as a separate, noncommunal dwelling. But with walls of adobe echoing the

rich tones and sculpted contours of the Southwestern landscape, the ties to nature remained
strong. Interiors welcomed their inhabitants
like a mother—indeed, the Earth Mother—
warmly wrapping her arms around a child.

To this day, the spirit of the Southwest
continues to inspire its architecture. Seen from
a distance, the city of Santa Fe resembles a
thriving native pueblo, thanks to building
ordinances that recognize the beauty of adobe.
Throughout the region, contemporary homes
adapt the native vernacular, incorporating
nichos and beehive fireplaces into soaring
rooms with walls of glass that frame the
landscape.

No matter how sophisticated the architecture
of the contemporary Southwestern home, this
simple yet profound verse of the Navajo people
expresses the inextricable connection between the
structure and its surroundings:

House made of dawn
House made of evening light.
House made of the dark cloud.
House made of male rain.
House made of dark mist.
House made of female rain.
House made of pollen.
House made of grasshoppers.
Dark cloud is at the door.
The trail out of it is dark cloud.
The zigzag lightning stands high upon it.

12

The people of the Southwest have always lived in close harmony with the region's rugged landscape. During the thirteenth century, Pueblo tribes built and then abandoned dwellings in the steep canyon walls at what is now called Mesa Verde, Colorado (page 10). Even modern architecture, like Santa Fe's Inn at Loretto (left), takes inspiration from native architecture; and contemporary adobe homes, such as the one shown below, left, are built from earthen bricks following a centuries-old practice.

14

CLIFF DWELLINGS: SCULPTED BY NATURE AND MAN

All over the Southwest, dwellings ranging in age from roughly seven hundred
to well over a thousand years old may
be seen high on rocky cliffsides. Among
the earliest extant dwellings of the
region, they provide us with a profound—if still sometimes puzzling—
insight into the close harmony with
nature that pervades local architecture
to this day.

A first glimpse of one such dwelling—
be it at Mesa Verde, Colorado; Montezuma Castle in Arizona; Bandelier
National Monument near Santa Fe,
New Mexico; or others scattered
throughout the area—may seem like an
optical illusion, as if the face of the cliff
had subtly reshaped itself before your
eyes, forming an intricate pattern of
walls, doorways, and windows. Blink
again, you fear, and they all will vanish.

This imagined possibility, in fact, is
not far from the truth. Over millions of
years, the rivers that carved out the

Southwest's vast valley plains worked along with the wind to erode deep caves in the sides of mesas composed of limestone, sandstone, or other porous rock. Beginning late in the first millennium, prehistoric peoples of the region began to move from their ground-based homes into these penthouses, which offered such advantages as protection from predators and enemies, extra shelter both from the harsh desert heat and occasional flooding, awe-inspiring views, and, no doubt, a feeling of living close to Mother Earth. Using fallen rocks as well as blocks pried or cut from the surroundings, these tribes erected walls to close off their homes from the elements. Following the contours of the cliff face, these walls seem almost to restore what nature herself had swept away.

Mysteriously, the cliff dwellings were abandoned by the mid-fifteenth century, and the peoples who built them—the Anasazi, the Hohokam, the Sinagua—were assimilated into other tribes. Many reasons have been put forward to explain the desertion, including malnutrition, disease, and changes in climate. In all likelihood, a combination of these factors worked together.

But the cliff dwellings themselves endure. And images of them are never far from the mind when one regards even the most contemporary Southwestern homes. They suggest that the ideal home allows the dweller to live in close contact with the planet.

Father Vaillant's mind was full of material cares as he approached Manuel Lujon's place beyond Bernalillo. The rancho was like a little town, with all its stables, corrals, and stake fences. The casa grande was long and low, with glass windows and bright blue doors, a portale running its full length, supported by blue posts. Under this portale the adobe wall was hung with bridles, saddles, great boots and spurs, guns and saddle blankets, strings of red peppers, fox skins, and the skins of two great rattlesnakes.

—Willa Cather, Death Comes for the Archbishop

15

HOMES AND INTERIORS

Some Cliff Dwellings of Note

A wealth of magnificent cliff dwellings stands ready to receive visitors at national parks and monuments throughout the Southwest. Some recommendations:

Bandelier National Monument, off of U.S. 285, near Los Alamos, north of Santa Fe, New Mexico. More rugged and ancient dwellings carved into a volcanic cliffside. The monument also includes hiking trails and summer moonlight tours.

Chaco Culture National Historic Park, on N.M. 57, between Blanco Trading Post and Thoreau, northeast of Gallup, New Mexico. Commonly known as Chaco Canyon, these vast Anasazi ruins carved into sandstone cliffs are famed for the precipitous prehistoric road system that connects the various pueblos. Four self-guided trails and a visitor center are supplemented by guided tours in the summer.

Canyon de Chelly National Monument, off of U.S. 191, on the Navajo Reservation near Chinle, Arizona. Perhaps the most dramatic cliff dwellings in the Southwest, near the foot of spectacular gorges, with cliffs that soar as high as a thousand feet above them. Expeditions into the canyon are led by Navajo guides or park rangers.

Mesa Verde National Park, off of U.S. 160 between Cortez and Durango, Colorado. Generally acknowledged to be the finest and most extensive ruins and, for that reason, a major attraction. Park rangers lead visitors on extensive tours of the cliff dwellings, most of which were not only built but also abandoned during the thirteenth century. A highlight is a look into the largest and most magnificent of the ruins, the four-story-tall Cliff Palace, composed of 217 separate rooms.

Montezuma Castle National Monument, on Interstate 17, between Phoenix and Flagstaff, Arizona. Small and very well preserved dwellings built around A.D. 1000 and originally inhabited by about fifty people. No direct access to the dwellings, but an excellent visitor's center and nature trail provide vivid information and lovely views.

Tonto National Monument, off of U.S. 60, east of Phoenix, Arizona. Situated at the base of sheer cliffs that stand above a steep slope studded with saguaro cacti, these early-fourteenth-century dwellings present a somewhat less startling but still fascinating prospect than those at the better-known monuments. A self-guided trail leads visitors to the lower ruins, and tour guides—booked in advance—give access to the upper dwellings.

Named for noted Southwestern ethnologist and novelist, Adolph Bandelier, the cliff dwellings of Bandelier National Monument (opposite), near Los Alamos, New Mexico, were built and occupied from the early thirteenth to the early seventeenth century A.D. Near Chinle, Arizona, the precipitous red sandstone cliffs and gorges of Canyon de Chelly (above) form a magnificent setting for ruins estimated to date back as far as A.D. 306.

ADOBE:
LIVING IN THE EARTH

Frank Lloyd Wright, whose own architecture found tremendous inspiration in the Southwest (see page 24), may well have coined the term *organic architecture*. But perhaps no dwelling, past or present, is more organic than the quintessential Southwestern adobe.

What other buildings take their names, plain and simple, from the materials of which they are made? The term *adobe* (of Arabic derivation, and brought here by the Spanish) applies, first and foremost, to the earth itself—moistened and then layered and dried repeatedly to build up walls of what is known as "coursed" or "puddle" adobe. Hand-shaped bricks, dried in the sun and then layered with muddy mortar, brought more sophistication to the building process, and the Spaniards improved it further by introducing wooden molds into which the mud—mixed with straw for greater strength and easier drying—was packed. Present-day commercial adobe yards add stabilizers to their bricks to help

them resist moisture, and thus last longer.

Whatever the kind of adobe used, the houses made from them are also called adobes. Covered with adobe plaster or with stucco, they exhibit the soft, irregular, organic contours of the earth itself. And they tend to grow organically, with one basically square or rectangular room tacking itself onto the next in a straight line, an L, or a U shape. There are few if any inner hallways, for their doorways open instead onto a common veranda—the *portal*—and, in larger homes, a central courtyard.

For stability and insulation against the harsh desert climate, the adobe's walls are thick. In some cases they are even composed of two parallel walls to make what is known as a "double adobe." Cool in summer, warm in winter, and always quiet, an adobe comes as close to the feeling of living safe and sheltered within the bosom of the earth as humans can get above ground.

Adobe Variations

To the untrained eye, an adobe is
an adobe is an adobe. In actuality,
however, the adobe dwelling has
evolved over the years into three
broad styles that, while bearing
the similarities of their common
origin, also show off distinctive
differences.

Hacienda

High adobe walls surrounding a spacious front courtyard and the adobe
house characterize this style, which
provided a safe haven to ranchers who
suffered repeated attacks by the Navajo,
Apache, and Comanche tribes. As the
heart of large, working ranches, such
homes were often built on a grander
scale, with higher ceilings and more
spacious floor plans.

Ranch

Dwellings built in the ranch style of the
late nineteenth century testify to the
decreasing fears of Indian attack. Like
the so-called ranch-style houses of our
own times, these adobe dwellings tend
to sprawl—taking full advantage of the
wide-open spaces in which they were
built—with spacious porches and
rooms generously open to the daylight.
Being far off in the countryside, they
also tend to be more rustic, displaying
weathered wood and interiors more
roughly finished than city or town
homes. And they also betray the influence of settlers from back East, who
brought with them a fondness for
board or log walls that combine with,
or sometimes altogether replace, the
adobe.

Territorial

With the opening of the Santa Fe Trail
in the early 1820s, the Southwest was
opened up to the U.S. influence—
which grew only stronger when New
Mexico became a U.S. territory after
the Mexican-American War in 1846.
The so-called territorial style of adobe
home reflects this influence in a number of significant details, from pitched
tin roofs to spacious double-hung windows, elaborate woodwork trim to
interior hallways that betray a more
European layout.

A*dobe is
ubiquitous in
the Southwest. It is
found in simple struc-
tures like the outdoor
ovens—known by
their Spanish name,
hornos—that are
used for baking in the
pueblos (opposite).
And the smooth,
rounded contours of
adobe houses, typi-
fied by the Abiquiu,
New Mexico, home
of legendary artist
Georgia O'Keeffe
(above), are the hall-
mark of indigenous
architecture.*

20

Taos Pueblo: A Living Architectural Monument

As a designated World Heritage site, Taos Pueblo ranks with the Great Pyramid at Giza and the Mayan temples at Chichén Itzá. And just as those other monuments seem to dominate the architectural consciousness of their respective nations, so too in its way does Taos Pueblo embody the very essence of what we now call Southwestern architecture.

Once you've seen the main five-story building at Taos, its image will reverberate in the mind whenever you regard an adobe dwelling: the stepped-back multiple levels; the gently curved corners; the recessed, painted wooden doorways; the vigas (ceiling beams) jutting out just below the roof line; the adobe walls themselves, with bits of straw catching the sunlight and glinting like strands of gold amid the dried earth. You'll even find new Southwestern structures that pay direct tribute to the pueblo: one major case in point is Santa Fe's Inn at Loretto, a hotel whose modern archi-

tecture is a striking abstraction of the five-century-old original.

Even more stunning than Taos's architecture itself is the fact that it—along with another, less distinctive four-story structure on the south side of the pueblo—remains to this day inhabited by some one thousand descendants of the people who built the structure around A.D. 1450, and who have lived at or near that site for almost a thousand years. Now, as then, the building is divided into self-contained, two-room family apartments, with a front room devoted to living and sleeping, and a back room to cooking, eating, and storage. Communal areas include outdoor domed ovens—*hornos*—and subterranean chambers known as *kivas,* which are used for religious ceremonies.

Such sacred places are off limits to outsiders, though the rest of the pueblo is open daily to members of the public, who pay a small fee. Throughout the year, though, visitors are welcome to witness various tribal dances connected with their traditional observances. Like the pueblo itself, they offer rare glimpses into a past whose spirit still shapes the Southwest.

MODERN SOUTHWESTERN HOMES

All over the Southwest today, as well as farther afield, architects and interior designers are reinterpreting the historic elements of local adobe dwellings in boldly innovative new homes that take advantage of modern building materials and engineering methods. The result is a striking contemporary version of Southwestern architecture that nevertheless springs from and adapts to the environment, in its way, as naturally as the cliff dwellings emerge from the rock at Canyon de Chelly or the pueblo rises to salute the Sangre de Cristo range at Taos.

The effects architects achieve vary according to the individual's tastes and backgrounds. In the Catalina Foothills of Tucson, architect Ron Fridland, AIA, designed an adobe-colored frame-and-stucco house that, from the front, resembles a clean-lined, square-cornered abstraction of a traditional dwelling. Its living spaces, however, take in the desert scenery through ceiling-high walls of glass. Drawing on tradition in a different way, architect Charles Foreman Johnson constructed an adobe-style dwelling (using reinforced concrete) on a hillside strewn with gigantic granite boulders in Carefree, Arizona. The building merges with the terrain, incorporating the massive rocks into its structure. The entire house,

including its ceiling of *vigas* and *latillas*, is scaled far larger than tradition would dictate, to match the surroundings.

The appeal of Southwestern architecture reaches beyond geographical boundaries. In Rancho Mirage, California, the Palm Desert architecture team of Richard Holden, AIA, and William Carl Johnson, AIA, collaborated with interior designer Steve Chase on his new home, which features a ceiling of redwood strips resembling a streamlined version of *latillas*, and a poolside gazebo whose glass-block walls are stepped like the walls of an adobe dwelling.

A sense of place has always been integral to Southwestern architecture. On the Taos mesa, a contemporary home by Albuquerque architect Antoine Predock echoes, in its stepped two-story form and its steeply angled roofs, the backdrop of the Sangre de Cristos and by extension nearby Taos Pueblo. An interior hallway, filled with light from a wall of windows, resembles a traditional *portal*, and its walls are painted a rich terra-cotta color.

Within such homes, myriad design effects might be found. Round-cornered adobe fireplaces towering two stories high in living rooms with vaulted ceilings. Elaborate arrangements of *nichos* specifically designed to display extensive collections of Native American art. Doors or gates of copper, bronze, or cast iron, displaying modern abstractions of ancient Indian motifs. Large, streamlined windows deftly etched in the blue paint of Santa Fe or Taos. Such are the many small details that compose the modern picture of Southwestern architecture.

Traditional Southwestern architecture can appear surprisingly contemporary, as with this recently built adobe home near Santa Fe (opposite). An older regional dwelling (above), showcases a Native American rug, Spanish-style wooden furniture, santos, and vigas.

At his Scottsdale, Arizona, headquarters, Taliesin West (above), Frank Lloyd Wright randomly incorporated local stones into his low-lying structure. On a desert mesa midway between Phoenix and Flagstaff, Italian architect Paolo Soleri and his followers are building Arcosanti (opposite, top and bottom), their working model for a self-sufficient city.

Frank Lloyd Wright and Paolo Soleri

You can't travel the Southwest, particularly in Arizona, without soon hearing about or coming across the works of two of the greatest innovators in Southwestern architecture—neither of whom was born in the region. The late Frank Lloyd Wright, preeminent giant of modern architecture, was raised in Wisconsin and got his first major architectural experience in Chicago; and Paolo Soleri—who has also been called the leading architect of our time—was born and educated in Turin, Italy.

But both men were attracted to the Southwest's dramatic landscape and climate and responded to it with such astonishing creativity that they have forever changed not merely how we think about architecture but also, in some subtle ways, how we view the region.

Designed in 1937, Taliesin West, outside of Scottsdale, Arizona, became the western winter home of the Taliesin Fellowship, Wright's architectural practice and school. Of the many buildings, both public and private, he designed in the region, it stands today as the prime Southwestern example of the master's "organic" approach to architecture. Its walls are made of what Wright called "desert rubblestone," in which large, randomly placed local stones show through the poured concrete that holds them together. The building's low, elongated form hugs its foothill position, beholding the desert valley below while respecting the majesty of the mountains that rise behind it, illustrating Wright's ideal of "the man-made building heightening the beauty of the desert and the desert more beautiful because of the building."

A dissenting disciple of Wright, Soleri espouses a theory he calls "arcology"—a dynamic integration of architecture and ecology that offers a bold alternative to contemporary urban sprawl. Arcosanti, his living laboratory of arcology, has been under construction since 1970 on a desert mesa near Cordes Junction, Arizona, about sixty-five miles north of Phoenix. A handful of volunteers live there full-time, leading tours, working on the continuing construction, and casting Soleri-designed wind bells of bronze or ceramic that are sold worldwide to support Soleri's project as well as raise money for other worthwhile causes. While Arcosanti's futuristic geometric forms seem in many ways to challenge the landscape more than to complement it, they are, nevertheless, made from the local earth and from concrete. What's more, the buildings at Arcosanti are, like all of Soleri's work, specifically designed to be energy efficient and self-sufficient within the desert environment, making them, according to an article in *Newsweek*, "As urban architecture…probably the most important experiment undertaken in our lifetime."

© Lois Ellen Frank

© Lois Ellen Frank

A lengthy visual vocabulary characterizes Southwestern architecture, from massive adobe walls (opposite, left) to jutting canales and elaborate shutters (opposite, right) to the bright colors that frequently bring weather-beaten doorways vibrantly to life (left).

Doorways

Most often made of wood, in simple or elaborate arrangements of boards and slats, Southwestern doors are notable for their weathered appearance or, conversely, their bright colors. Blue seems to predominate—a color that, it is believed, blesses the house and wards off evil spirits.

Fireplaces

In living rooms and kitchens, fireplaces also grow organically from the adobe walls, frequently at a corner of the room. The most common shape of fireplace is the cone or beehive, sometimes referred to as a *kiva,* after the shape of Pueblo Indians' sacred underground ceremonial chambers.

Floors

Early adobes had floors of packed earth, as undulant as the walls. Later times have seen floors of wood planks, flagstone, brick, or terra-cotta tiles—particularly Mexican *saltillas.*

Gates

Like doorways, gates of wood—sometimes embellished with wrought iron—provide security while offering the opportunity to greet visitors with a particularly stylish and colorful flourish.

Ladders

Originally, ladders were the main means of entry into pueblo dwellings, which—for security's sake—offered no doorways on the ground floor. Some contemporary Southwestern homes still sport rough wooden ladders—both for decorative purposes and as a means of access to the roof for maintenance.

Latillas

In a common ceiling treatment, these stripped saplings or saguaro cactus ribs are laid side by side—perpendicularly or at an angle—across the beams.

Nichos

Open recesses built into the interior adobe walls, these serve the practical purpose of providing storage and, more and more today, the decorative purpose of displaying folk art and other prized possessions.

Placitas

These charming inner courtyards—whether brick lined or planted with simple gardens—provide a quiet center to the house that connects it with the outdoors.

Plaster

Interior walls and occasionally ceiling coves between the beams are coated in white plaster, which brightens the interior and contrasts with the earthiness of the adobe and the vivid colors of decorative artifacts.

Portales

Extensive covered porches or verandas, these run along the length of adobe homes, extending their living space outdoors. In some larger dwellings, portales appear on all four sides so that, depending on the season, there will always be a clement outdoor spot—cool and shady in summer, warm and sunny in winter.

Vigas

These massive ceiling beams—whole trees stripped of their bark—support the roof and extend outward through the house's walls.

Windows

Frames and shutters are treated in similar fashion to doors and gates—either weathered or brightly painted.

Cozy as a traditional Southwestern dwelling may be, the great outdoors is never far away. In a charming little inner courtyard or placita (opposite, below), a rustic bench and earthen jugs bring a homey atmosphere to the open air. A portal (opposite, top) provides a natural extension of the home's living space. Sunshine streams through the picture window of a stylish adobe with a ceiling supported by vigas (above).

Today's amateur or professional decorator has a wealth of Southwestern objects at his or her disposal, ranging from contemporary rugs displaying traditional Native American patterns and symbols (above) to a wealth of old-fashioned and contemporary decorative items (opposite)—including painted furniture, a kiva-style ladder, fanciful ironwork, and a folk-art snake.

SOUTHWESTERN FURNITURE: FROM SPAIN VIA MEXICO

You've heard the modern catchphrase that goes something like, "It's so old, it's new." That about sums up the continuing appeal of Southwestern furniture.

The style dates way back to the sixteenth century, when Spanish settlers traveled northward from Mexico City to the New Mexico Territory. They carried with them traditional Spanish-style furniture fashioned with New World materials: large, square-cornered pieces in cottonwood, pine, and juniper, sometimes decorated with intricately carved designs.

Not surprisingly, such simple lines look completely at home in the adobe dwellings of the Southwest, and they endure to this day in lovingly preserved antiques as well as in modern-day pieces that take their inspiration from those of the past—right down to nail-free joinery with mortises, tenons, dovetails, and dowels. Leading furniture manufacturing companies such as Drexel Heritage, Lane, and Thomasville have also joined in with their own Southwestern Spanish designs.

Vividly colored contemporary upholstery in native patterns may now adorn chair cushions. And a late-twentieth-century playfulness may occasionally find its way into the decorative detailing—particularly in pieces created by such designers as Jim Wagner, Ivory Crowley, Pete Chavez, and Frances Perea, who adorn their traditional-looking cupboards, mirrors, chairs, and other furnishings with local motifs that display a charming, childlike whimsy. But such variations and elaborations never conceal the stalwart forms beneath them. Now, as in the past, the four-hundred-year-old Spanish style is an integral part of the authentic Southwestern interior.

Elements of Southwestern Decor

Apart from the obvious architectural details and traditional furnishings, myriad elements may play a part in creating a Southwestern ambience in the home. Here are a few suggestions:

© Robert Reck

ometimes one
or a few well-
chosen Southwestern
objects can make the
most profound deco-
rative statement in
the home. Local
religious artifacts
(opposite) display the
profound power of
their forthright, devo-
tional craftsmanship.
A recently fashioned
polychrome jar (left),
dating from the
1910s or 1920s
and made in San
Ildefonso Historic
Pueblo, is decorated
with geometric sym-
bols that echo many
centuries of Native
American tradition.

Cacti

Whether small specimens on a window
ledge or large varieties in a pot on the
floor, cacti bring the desert indoors.

Candles

The soft glow of candlelight wonderfully complements the color and contours of adobe walls, and in any room
harkens back to earlier, more rustic
times. Votive candles are indispensable,
particularly in Southwestern homes in
which religious artifacts such as *santos*
are displayed.

Dried corn

Their husks still attached, small or large
ears of dried Indian corn add rich color
and texture, whether hung on the wall
or displayed on tabletops, shelves, or
mantels.

Hispanic artifacts

From carved wooden *santos* to religious
or secular tinwork to today's popular
folk art animals, objects expressing the
Southwest's Spanish heritage are frequent decorative elements in the home.

Native American artifacts

Likewise, a wide range of traditional
Native American artifacts from Hopi
kachinas to Navajo jewelry to Pueblo
pottery, make stunningly beautiful and
culturally significant additions to the
home.

Ranch hardware

Ranch-style adobe homes frequently
display the daily hardware of working
life—spurs, bells, bridles, buckles, plow-
shares, and the like—as decorative elements hung from the walls or placed on
shelves or mantels.

Ristras

Hung indoors and out, on walls and
from rafters, in living rooms as well
as kitchens, these strings of dried red
chiles may well be the single most
widely used decorative element in the
Southwestern home. At Christmastime, they're sometimes integrated into
holiday wreaths.

Rugs and other textiles

A subgroup of Native American artifacts deserving of special mention, vividly hued and eye-catchingly patterned
textiles are one of the most dependable,
effective ways to introduce color and
texture into the home. While Navajo
rugs are most common and authentic,
the use of Latin American weavings,
Asian kilims or other textiles, or even
New England or other early-American
quilts can achieve similar effects in contemporary homes.

Skulls

Georgia O'Keeffe's skull paintings may well have brought this element to the forefront of public consciousness. Sunbleached animal skulls—particularly of steers—are a natural occurrence in the desert ranchlands of the Southwest. While some people may practice a particularly grisly form of decorative over-kill by displaying a wide array of skulls, a single specimen makes a dramatically arresting focal point for a room.

Southwestern symbols

Steer skull. Howling coyote. Saguaro. Chile. Writhing snake. Such images have achieved an almost iconographic status in the Southwest. You'll find them in classic folk art and as contemporary decorative motifs—a neon cactus, perhaps, or a string of red chile Christmas lights. New variations on these visual themes seem to crop up almost daily; in the end, you're the judge on whether they cross the border from good taste into kitsch.

The sunbleached steer skull has become one of the preeminent symbols of the region.

SOUTHWESTERN FOODS

The centuries-old tradition of Southwestern cooking is finally getting some respect. Since prehistoric times, corn and beans have sustained the native people of the region, while the chile sparked their palates with its fire. Yet until recently, it seemed as if you had to apologize for eating the food that many people thought was "Mexican." It was considered by many people outside of the Southwest to be just one cut above junk food. No one took it very seriously.

But now, Southwestern restaurants thrive in major cities far removed from the Four Corners. Southwestern cookbooks sell at a chile-hot pace. Southwestern-style tableware appears in the most chic designer showrooms.

Why the sudden change in attitude? In fact, a number of factors seem to be at work here. The Southwest in general is enjoying an ever-growing popularity—both as a travel destination and as a style source. People from around the country and around the world visit the region and spend a few days eating its authentic dishes. And they like what they eat.

In recent years most people have also achieved a new level of sophistication about eating—not the false sophistication of someone whose palate can only appreciate the hautest cuisines, but rather a refined sense of appreciation for honest, interesting cooking, wherever it may be found. And there's a wealth of honest, delicious dishes coming from Southwestern kitchens.

That openness to new culinary experiences has had a profound effect as well on some of the nation's most innovative young chefs, who have discovered or rediscovered Southwestern cooking in their own professional pursuits of excellence, reinterpreting old dishes in exciting new ways.

Finally, there's the issue of health to consider. Recent medical findings have taught us that the diets of Western man and woman have gone sadly, dangerously astray. But the foods of Southwestern people are rich in the very things we're now learning are good for us: complex carbohydrates and dietary fiber. As the twentieth century draws to its close, corn and beans have never looked so good!

R obust, simple, sometimes fiery flavors characterize the basic foods of the Southwest—including beans and chiles (page 36) and the all-important staple, corn, shown here in the form of dried Indian hominy.

39

*F*resh or dried, chiles are the seasoning of choice in the Southwest. Long braided strings or ristras (below) of red Anaheim chiles dry in the hot New Mexican sun. Roasted until their shiny skins blacken and blister, fresh green chiles are then carefully peeled (opposite) before use.

If you had to select one food as the defining characteristic of the Southwestern kitchen, it would have to be the chile. Dried and pulverized to make chile powder; simmered and puréed to yield the region's two signature sauces, Chile Colorado and Chile Verde (see pages 42-43); roasted, seeded, and stuffed for a classic Chiles Rellenos (see page 44); or chopped raw in a fresh salsa (see page 45): chiles pervade the region's cuisine, enlivening it with their subtle—or not so subtle—fire.

While dozens of varieties and subvarieties of chiles exist around the world, Southwestern cooks rely on a few main standbys:

Anaheim It's the region's definitive chile. When it is still green, it's known as the long green chile or the *chile verde*. Ripened to red, it's called—not surprisingly—the red chile or *chile colorado*, which is often seen dried and tied together by the stems in the long decorative strands known as *ristras*. The heat will vary with the exact strain and where and how it was grown, with the chile ranging from mild to hot. Canned green chiles, a fairly mild product, are usually Anaheims.

Ancho Also known as the *poblano*, this chile looks like a tapered version of a bell pepper, and is mild to hot in strength. Fresh and green, it is often used for making *chiles rellenos*. Brick-red dried anchos have a rich, smoky flavor.

Jalapeño This shiny-skinned, plump little green pepper is a killer in the heat category. It's always used fresh and is widely available year round.

Serrano As hot as the jalapeño, but with a somewhat less sharp flavor, the short, skinny serrano is used fresh to season salsas and even guacamole.

Hot to Handle

The quickest, easiest way to roast and peel chiles is the hot-oil method. In a deep, heavy skillet, heat a few inches of vegetable oil to about 400 degrees F on a deep-frying thermometer. Using long metal tongs, hold a chile by its stem and immerse it in the hot oil until its skin is evenly blistered, but less than 1 minute. Then drop the chile in a bowl of ice water and leave it while you repeat with the remaining chiles.

One by one, peel the blistered skin from the chiles. Slit them open along one side with the tip of a small, sharp knife and remove their seeds and white veins. If you'll be stuffing the chiles, as for Chiles Rellenos (see page 44), leave the stems attached; if not, remove them. The chiles are ready for use in any recipe.

Caution: *The fiery taste of chiles comes from volatile oils that readily adhere to your hands. If you have any cuts on your hands, you may want to wear kitchen gloves when handling chiles to avoid any painful burning. Likewise, take great care not to touch your eyes after you've handled chiles; wash your hands very thoroughly with lots of soap and water when done.*

Chile Verde
(Basic Green Chile Sauce)

You'll find this sauce frequently served over enchiladas or burritos in the Southwest, as well as used condiment style like its culinary cousin, chile colorado. Though this sauce has some bite to it, by no means is it overpowering. If you'd like to really fire up your tastebuds, you might want to add one or two chopped jalapeño peppers.

1/4 cup vegetable oil

1/2 pound good-quality stewing beef with a little fat, cut into 1/2-inch cubes

2 medium garlic cloves, finely chopped

12 Anaheim chiles, roasted and peeled (see instructions on page 41) but not seeded, finely chopped

1 to 2 cups water

Salt

In a skillet over medium heat, heat the oil and then sauté the beef until it is browned and cooked through. Remove the meat and set it aside, draining well and leaving a tablespoon or two of oil in the skillet.

Over the heat, put the garlic in the pan and sauté just until it sizzles, without browning. Add the chiles and the meat, and stir in enough water to give it a pourable sauce consistency; reduce the heat and simmer gently for about 20 minutes, stirring in more water as necessary. Season to taste before serving.

Makes 4 to 5 cups

Chile Colorado
(Basic Red Chile Sauce)

This brick-red elixir is, in tandem with chile verde, a fundamental sauce of Southwestern cuisine, turning up in enchiladas, over burritos and chiles rellenos and tamales, seasoning stews, saucing meats and poultry, and even served in a bowl as a sort of condiment. (Try it over your scrambled eggs at breakfast—it's sensational!) While many variations exist, and the taste will vary somewhat with the crop of chiles you use, this basic recipe will serve you well.

1/2 pound dried whole New Mexican red chiles, or medium-hot New Mexican red chile powder

1 1/2 medium garlic cloves, finely chopped

6 cups (plus extra) chicken stock, pork stock, or water

Salt

If you're using whole chiles, remove the stems and seeds (see the cautionary note on page 41). Place the whole chiles in a hot oven, about 400 degrees F, and roast several minutes until they darken, turning them frequently and taking care that they don't burn.

Put the chiles or the powder in a blender with the garlic and the stock. Blend until smooth. Transfer to a saucepan and cook over medium heat until the sauce just begins to bubble, adding salt and more stock if necessary to keep it fairly fluid. Sieve and season to taste.

Makes 4 to 5 cups

Setting the Southwestern Table

For stylish Southwestern entertaining, a wide range of options—both old-fashioned and newfangled—are available to transform the home dining table.

If you've got a good-looking wooden or slate table, let it show. Or cover your table with a contemporary, inexpensive weaving or tablecloth inspired by traditional Native American patterns, complementing it with similar napkins in Southwestern colors and patterns.

For tableware, plain glazed terracotta is a good way to go, to reflect the earth tones of the region itself and complement the rich colors of the cuisine. Contemporary Native American, Hispanic, and Anglo craftspeople are also making remarkable glazed dishes, platters, bowls, and pitchers that sport traditional tribal designs or hip renderings of cacti, lizards, birds, and other creatures. And a number of commercial dishware manufacturers are also following suit, offering patterns and colors inspired by the Southwest.

To decorate the table, select one or more of your favorite and appropriate Southwestern handiworks—be it a folk-art chicken or pig, a squash kachina, or a santo depicting San Pascual Baylón (patron saint of the kitchen, of course). You might also like to choose a special piece such as a single beautiful Native American pot or bowl—bearing in mind that you run the risk of it being knocked over and damaged. Or lay out a beautiful arrangement of traditional ingredients—say, a grouping of dried ears of colored corn, or a beautiful ristra of red chiles. And to light the table, plain or glazed pottery candlesticks are widely available, as are craftsman-made wrought-iron versions reminiscent of the ranch tradition.

Christmas-Style Burrito

No, this isn't a traditional Christmas dish. The name came from a waitress at a Southwestern dive who, when faced with a customer who couldn't choose between having red or green chile on his burrito, said impatiently, "Honey, why dontcha have it both ways, Christmas-style?" The combination is great.

The name burrito—"little burro"— probably comes from the fact that, like that sturdy pack animal, a flour tortilla can carry quite a heavy load. You can elaborate on the filling, if you like, with your choice of meat, poultry, or even seafood.

4 large flour tortillas

2 cups hot Refries without the cheese (see page 59)

6 ounces shredded Monterey Jack cheese

6 ounces shredded sharp Cheddar cheese

1 cup Guacamole (see page 59)

2 cups warm Chile Colorado (see page 43)

2 cups warm Chile Verde (see page 42)

Briefly warm the tortillas on both sides on a hot griddle.

Place each tortilla on a flat work surface. Spread the hot refries evenly across the center of each burrito. Sprinkle the cheeses evenly over the beans, then dot dollops of the guacamole on top.

Fold in the edges of each tortilla about 1 inch over the filling. Then fold the side nearest to you over the filling and carefully roll up the burrito.

Place each burrito on a heated serving plate. Ladle the red chile over one end of each burrito, and the green over the other, so that the 2 sauces meet in the middle.

Serves 4

Beer-Battered Chiles Rellenos

Using beer in the batter gives a fuller, richer flavor to these classic favorites, whose name means simply "stuffed chiles."

2 eggs, separated

1 cup all-purpose flour

3/4 cup beer

2 teaspoons cornstarch

1/2 teaspoon salt

Pinch of white pepper

8 long green Anaheim chiles, roasted, peeled, slit and seeded, stems left on (see instructions, page 41)

1/2 pound Monterey Jack cheese, cut into 8 equal chile-length strips

Oil for deep frying

2 to 4 cups Chile Colorado or Chile Verde (see pages 42–43)

In a processor or mixing bowl, combine the egg yolks, 3/4 cup of flour, the beer, cornstarch, salt, and pepper. Cover and leave at room temperature while you beat the egg whites to stiff but not dry peaks. Fold the whites into the batter.

Carefully stuff the chiles with the cheese.

In a heavy skillet or deep fryer, heat several inches of oil to 375 degrees F on a deep-frying thermometer.

Dredge each chile lightly with flour and dip it thoroughly in the batter, then carefully drop it into the oil. Fry, turning once with a skimmer, until golden brown, about 2 minutes. Drain on paper towels.

Serve with your choice of chile sauce, ladling about 1/2 cup per chile.

Serves 4 to 8

Salsa Fresca

"Even though I'm a gringo," confessed Tucson writer Tom Danehy in a recent article in the *Valley Guide Quarterly*, "I was fortunate enough to grow up in an ethnic area of L.A., so I knew about salsa from the jump. I put it on my Malt-o-Meal, mixed it into my Ovaltine, and rubbed it on my chest when we ran out of Vicks Vap-o-Rub. But mostly I dipped chips in it. For days at a time, that's all I would eat."

Truth be told, for many aficionados of Southwestern food, salsa amounts to nothing less than one of the basic food groups. In the following version of this basic table sauce—which, indeed, is a great dip for Tostaditas (see page 48) or condiment for just about anything savory you'd like to eat—the bite of fresh chiles combines with the sweet, mild flavor of tomatoes and the spark of other familiar Southwestern seasonings. Feel free to adjust the proportions to suit your own taste, and if you like a thinner salsa, stir in a little ice water before serving.

4 medium-sized, firm, ripe tomatoes, stemmed and halved, seeds squeezed out, coarsely chopped

1 small red onion, finely chopped

1 garlic clove, finely chopped

1 green Anaheim chile, stemmed, seeded, and finely chopped (see cautionary note on page 41)

6 tablespoons finely chopped fresh cilantro leaves

2 tablespoons fresh lime juice

Salt and freshly ground white or black pepper

In a mixing bowl, stir together all the ingredients, seasoning to taste. Cover and refrigerate at least 1 hour before serving.

Makes 2 to 3 cups

CORN: SUSTENANCE OF MANY COLORS

If wheat bread is the staff of life to most of Western civilization, then corn deserves that role in the Southwest. Whether eaten fresh or soaked with lime to make whole-kernel hominy—which is used to make Posole (see page 51; *posole* means hominy in Spanish), or dried and ground into masa flour for tortillas or tamales—corn appears at virtually every Southwestern meal.

To those who normally eat yellow or occasionally white corn, the signature blue-gray corn of the Southwest comes as a startling surprise. Its flavor bears out the promise of the color: earthier, richer, with a somewhat grittier texture.

And like the speckled pilgrim corn we're all familiar with from Thanksgiving decorations, Southwestern corn grows in other colors as well: reds, pinks, and blacks. Though you won't ordinarily find such corn sold commercially, its diversity is but one more example of the wealth that springs from a seemingly arid land.

But using that wealth isn't always easy. There are some tricks one needs to know before attempting to make two of the most popular corn dishes, tortillas and tamales.

Shaping Corn Tortillas

True residents of the Southwest seem to be able to pat balls of masa back and forth between their hands to shape perfectly round corn tortillas without a second thought. But for those who didn't grow up making tortillas in the family kitchen, the technique won't necessarily come easily.

There are several ways to get good, round tortillas. The simplest is to track down a local Mexican market that makes them up fresh or gets them in from a nearby small tortilla factory. (For that matter, you can visit the factory yourself.) Fresh tortillas freeze well when wrapped in airtight plastic bags.

Or you can buy a cast-iron tortilla press. Just put a ball of masa between two sheets of waxed paper in the press, lower the lid, and presto!

You can also use a small rolling pin to roll out the tortilla by hand between two sheets of waxed paper, though you're still likely to get irregularly shaped results.

And then there's the most devious, ingenious approach I've come across, revealed by Huntley Dent in his outstanding book *The Feast of Santa Fe.* He thinly rolls out the dough between two layers of heavy plastic film cut from ziplock freezer bags. Then he cuts out perfect, five- or six-inch rounds using a sharp-edged pot lid (he recommends Revere Ware lids as having just the right cutting properties!).

Corn Tortillas

Whichever way you shape the tortilla (see page 47), all that remains is to griddle-bake it—about 30 seconds per side—on a hot, cast-iron griddle or large skillet. The tortilla is then ready for eating or further cooking.

As for the masa dough you use to make the tortillas, its ingredients and preparation couldn't be simpler:

2 cups masa harina

1/4 teaspoon salt

1 to 1 1/4 cups warm water

In a mixing bowl, stir together the masa harina and salt. Stir in enough of the water to make a thick, firm, but soft dough. Shape immediately into tortillas.

Makes enough for about 1 dozen tortillas

Tostaditas

Maybe they're taco chips to most of us. But whatever you call them, these crisp-fried triangles of corn tortilla are a widespread favorite to munch on as a snack, to enjoy with drinks before a meal, to dip into salsa or guacamole, or to serve as a garnish to a main dish. Blue corn tostaditas make a delightful change from the usual yellow ones.

There are no quantities here, since you'll want to fry up fresh as many as you'll need. Just be sure to have a sufficient depth of oil, to have it at the right temperature, and not to overfill the pan with tortillas—all of which could lead to soggy, greasy chips.

Corn tortillas

Vegetable oil

Salt

Stack several tortillas at a time and, with a large, sharp knife, carefully cut them into 6 or 8 wedges each.

In a large, deep, heavy skillet or a deep fryer, heat 2 to 3 inches of oil to 360 degrees F on a deep-frying thermometer. Carefully scatter a batch of tortillas into the oil, taking care not to overcrowd the skillet. Fry until crisp and golden, about 1 minute, then remove with a wire strainer and drain on paper towels. Sprinkle with salt if you wish. Repeat with remaining tortillas, adding more oil if necessary and checking and adjusting the temperature between batches.

Flat Blue Corn Enchiladas

The tube-shaped rolled enchiladas most of us are familiar with are not the most authentic. These simple, flat versions are more like the way they were traditionally made in the Southwest.

1/4 to 1/2 cup vegetable oil

12 blue corn (or yellow corn) tortillas

*3 cups Chile Colorado (see page 43)
or canned enchilada sauce*

1/2 pound shredded Monterey Jack cheese

1/2 pound shredded sharp Cheddar cheese

1 medium red onion, finely chopped

2 medium scallions, finely chopped

4 eggs (optional)

Shredded iceberg lettuce

Preheat the broiler.

Heat 1/4 cup of the oil in a skillet over medium heat. Fry the tortillas one at a time for a few seconds each, just until soft; add more oil if necessary. Drain the tortillas on paper towels. Do not discard the oil.

Spread a spoonful or two of the chile on each of 4 ovenproof individual serving plates or casseroles just wider than a tortilla. Place a tortilla on each plate. Sprinkle with a third of the cheeses, half of the onions and scallions, and a little more chile. Repeat with another tortilla, another third of the cheese, the remaining onions and scallions, and more chile. Top with the last tortilla and the remaining chile, then finish with the remaining cheese.

Broil the enchiladas for several minutes on a middle rack of the broiler, not too close to the heat, until they're heated through and the cheese is bubbly. If you like, while they're broiling, fry the eggs sunny side up or over easy in the hot oil.

Carefully remove the plates from the oven, placing them on top of larger heat-proof servers. Garnish with the eggs, and scatter the lettuce around each stack.

Serves 4

Shaping Tamales

1. Soak the dried corn husks in hot water until soft, about 30 minutes. Reserve the good, whole ones; tear smaller or damaged ones into long strips.

2. Put a generous 1/4 cup of prepared masa into the center of each whole husk and spread it into a square about 1/2 inch thick.

3. Spoon about 2 tablespoons of the filling vertically down the center of the masa.

4. Using the sides of the husk, roll the masa up on both sides of the filling to enclose it.

5. Fold in the sides to enclose the tamale. Fold the top and bottom over to completely enwrap the package and use 1 or more of the husk strips to tie up the package securely.

Chicken and Green Chile Tamales

I find this to be a pleasant, light-tasting variation on the more conventional tamales filled with red meat and red chile.

1¹/₂ cups masa harina
(Mexican-style ground cornmeal)

1 teaspoon baking powder

1/4 cup vegetable shortening

2 tablespoons unsalted butter, softened

3/4 cup chicken broth, warmed

1/2 cup milk, warmed

Dried corn husks

1 cup shredded cooked white-meat chicken

Chile Verde (see page 42)

In a food processor with the metal blade, combine the masa, baking powder, shortening, and butter; pulse several times until they form a coarse meal. Combine the broth and milk and add 1 cup to the processor; process just until the mixture forms a thick but soft and spreadable dough, adding a little more liquid, if necessary. Transfer to a bowl, cover, and set aside.

Soak the corn husks. To make the filling, stir the chicken together with a little Chile Verde—just enough to moisten all the meat.

Shape the tamales as directed.

Cook the tamales in a steamer over boiling water for about 45 minutes. Remove from the steamer and let them cool for about 5 minutes before serving, allowing guests to unwrap them at table. Pass additional chile sauce on the side.

Serves 4

© Lois Ellen Frank

Posole

This traditional Southwestern soup-stew takes its name from the Spanish word for the whole hominy—large, hulled kernels of lime-soaked dried corn—that it is made of. It's most easily made with frozen posole—purchased in large supermarkets or Mexican shops—or the widely available canned whole hominy.

One of the greatest pleasures of the dish is its array of accompaniments, which each guest adds to his or her portion to taste.

3 tablespoons vegetable oil

1 large onion, finely chopped

2 garlic cloves, finely chopped

2 pounds lean pork stewing meat, cut into $^1/_2$-to-1-inch pieces

2 quarts or more cold water

2 whole dried red chiles

1 bay leaf

1 teaspoon dried oregano

$^1/_4$ teaspoon whole black peppercorns

$^1/_4$ teaspoon whole white peppercorns

$^1/_4$ teaspoon whole cumin seeds

$^1/_4$ teaspoon whole allspice

2 pounds frozen posole, simmered in lightly salted water for 1 hour, then drained; or 2 (29-ounce) cans whole hominy, drained

Salt to taste

Accompaniments

1 cup Chile Colorado (see page 43)

1 cup Chile Verde (see page 42)

1 cup thinly sliced radishes

1 cup thinly sliced scallions

$^1/_4$ cup dried oregano

2 ripe avocados, peeled, pitted, and coarsely chopped

2 limes, cut into quarters

Heat the oil in a large stockpot over medium heat, and sauté the onion and garlic until transparent. Add the pork and sauté until lightly browned. Then add the water, chiles, and all the seasonings and bring to a boil. Reduce the heat, cover, and simmer gently until the pork is just tender, about 2 hours.

Stir in the posole and add enough extra water to keep all the ingredients covered. Simmer about 1 hour more, until the posole and the pork are very tender.

Arrange all the accompaniments in separate bowls on the dining table. Ladle the posole into deep serving bowls and pass the accompaniments for guests to add to their servings.

Serves 4

BEANS AND OTHER BASICS

Beans, which dry conveniently for long-term storage, bring their abundant proteins and carbohydrates to the Southwestern diet. Sometimes mashed and fried in lard or oil to make refried beans, they are a popular side dish, and are often found spread on a flat, crisp tortilla to form the base of a tostada.

In *New Mexico Magazine's More of the Best from New Mexico Kitchens*, writer John Crenshaw contributes an eloquent "Paean to the Pinto Bean" and its role in the building of Southwestern civilization. He points out that corn, which tends to get more attention by those who regard the region's cuisine, was planted casually by early New Mexicans. "Beans," on the other hand, "took more tending, indicating the beginnings of a more settled life—perhaps even requiring it." Beans were eaten by ancient peoples more than a millennium and a half ago.

Today, as then, their combination of proteins and complex carbohydrates offers an ideal food to Southwesterners and to anyone else who appreciates their robust, earthy taste and texture. And as for their lengendary drawback? Crenshaw, as do many other experts, recommends long overnight soaking—with up to three water changes—to eliminate gas-causing compounds from beans. He also admits that the technique simply may not work, in which case you should "let its flaw pass."

Red flames and
blue smoke leaped up
through the trees as
the fires were started
for supper. Later the
people visited their
neighbors' camps
and sang and danced
in the silver moon-
light. When tired,
they stopped to sit
around the camp
fires and hear the
stories of the elders;
the children always
listened attentively.
—Cleofas M.
Jaramillo,
Shadows of
the Past

53

The Southwestern Pantry

Apart from the fundamentals already described, a large pantry-ful of other ingredients are essential to Southwestern cooking. Leaving out really basic ingredients like cheese and tomatoes that most contemporary kitchens have on hand, here are some of the more basic Southwestern ones you'll find yourself relying on:

Avocados

Peeled and sliced, or mashed up into guacamole, the buttery-textured fruit makes frequent appearances on Southwestern plates. Use only the bumpy-skinned Haas variety, which has the best flavor and texture: smooth, shiny-skinned types are hardly worth buying.

Chorizo

This spiced Mexican-style fresh pork sausage is sold in most Latin American food stores and in many large supermarkets. Be aware that in most cases the sausage will be raw, requiring peeling and cooking before it can be eaten.

Cilantro

Also known in some areas as green coriander or Chinese parsley, this fresh herb—which closely resembles flat-leafed Italian parsley—has a bright, spicy taste that sparks up dishes it garnishes.

Cumin

This musky, aromatic spice frequently flavors sauces and bean dishes.

Jicama

This large, knobby, brown-skinned root is one of the Southwest's most surprising vegetables. Thickly peeled, it reveals a watery, crisp interior that, eaten raw on its own or in salads, refreshes like an apple, with some of the texture and mildly sweet flavor of a water chestnut.

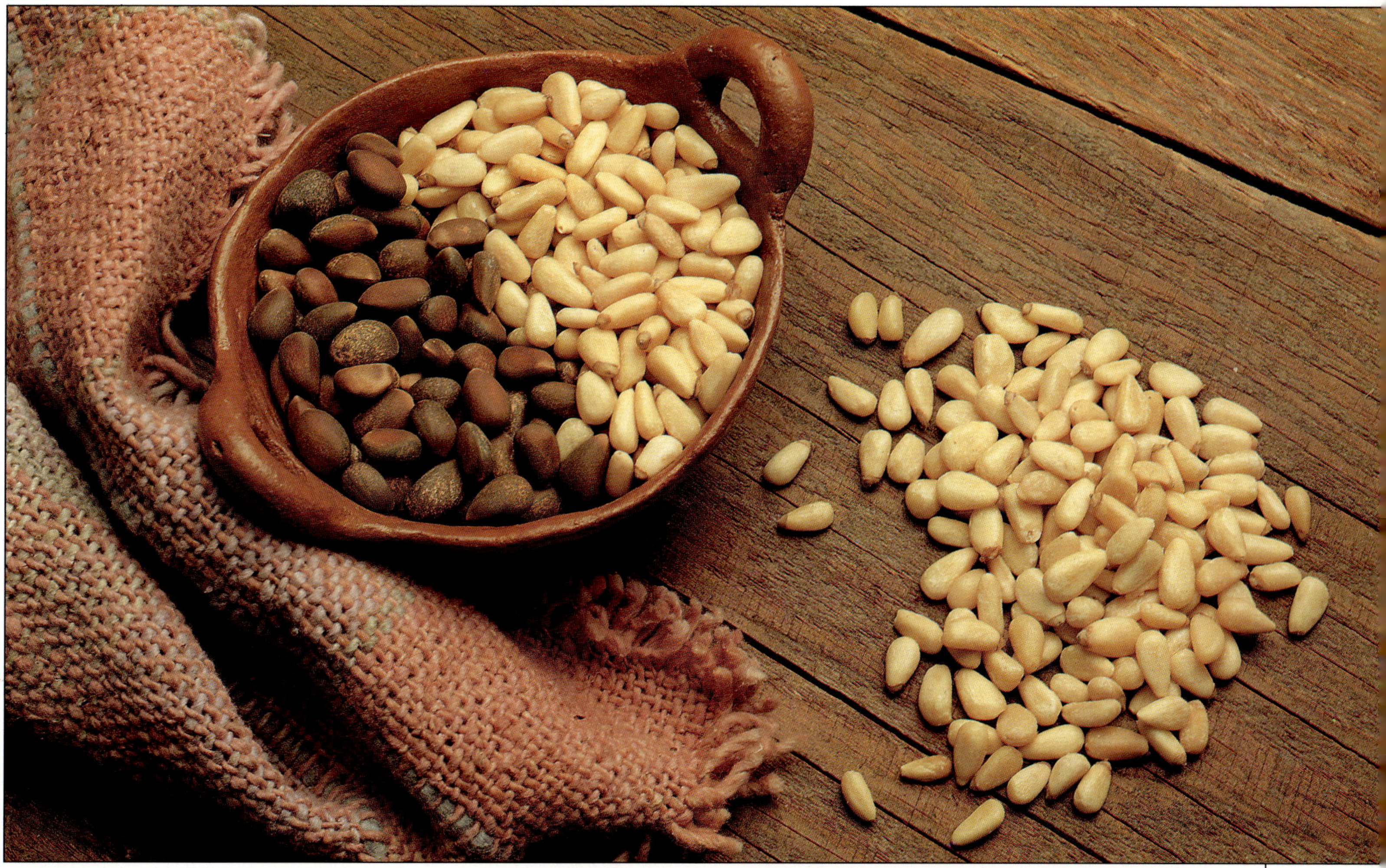

© Lois Ellen Frank

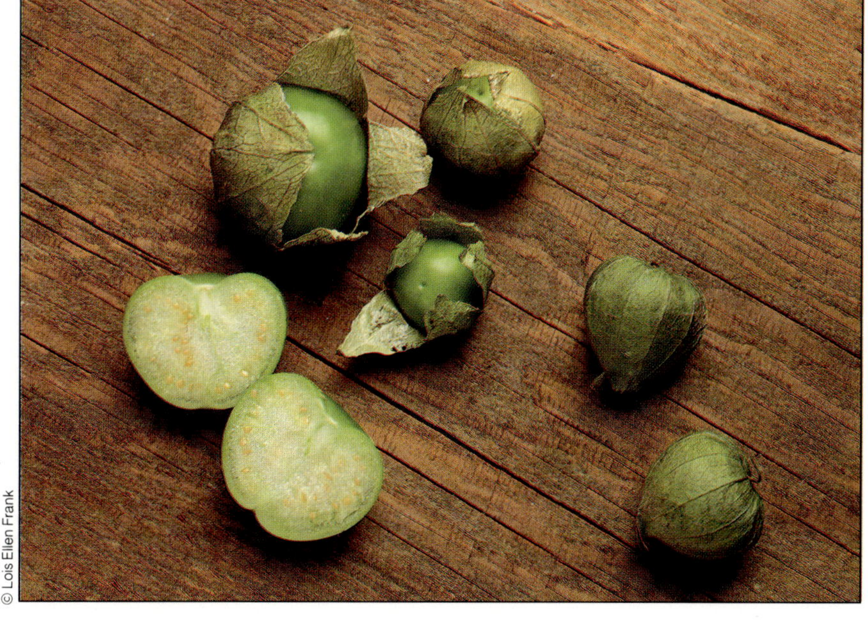

Piñones

Though most of the nation calls them pine nuts or pignolas, those terms raise steely-eyed frowns in the Southwest. These are excellent scattered in salads, mixed into pancake or waffle batters, and starring in a host of classic desserts and candies in which other nuts usually appear—from piñon pie to piñon brownies, piñon fudge to piñon brittle.

© Lois Ellen Frank

Tomatillos

Sometimes mistakenly called green tomatoes, these are in fact a different vegetable—though they do resemble tomatoes in shape, texture, and even flavor—with a mildly sharp and acidic taste. You'll find them covered in papery brown husks, which you peel off to reveal the shiny green skins beneath. Chopped up, they often appear raw or cooked in sauces.

Frijoles

You can use this basic formula to cook the Southwest's familiar pinto beans or the now-fashionable black beans that have worked their way north and westward from Mexican and Caribbean kitchens.

Just be aware that—depending on the kind of bean, how dry they are, how long they were stored, the kind of water you use, and no doubt other factors like the position of the stars in the heavens— you'll probably have to adjust the water and the cooking time, tasting and checking to make sure the beans are cooked through and completely tender.

2 cups pinto or black beans

2 quarts or more water

1/4 pound salt pork, rinsed and cut into 1/2-inch pieces

2 garlic cloves, finely chopped

1 small onion, finely chopped

2 to 4 teaspoons salt

The night before you cook them, carefully sort through the beans to remove any stones, bits of straw, or bad beans; rinse thoroughly. Put in a large bowl and cover with at least 6 cups of cold water (apart from the water listed in the ingredients). Leave to soak overnight at room temperature.

Drain the beans and rinse them well. Put them in a pot with the 2 quarts of water and bring to a boil. Stir in the salt pork, garlic and onion. Simmer gently, covered, until tender, 2 to 4 hours or so, adding more water as necessary to keep the beans from drying out. When the beans are done, season to taste with salt; they'll need a lot.

Serve as a side dish, plain or garnished with Chile Verde or Chile Colorado (see pages 42–43), or use in other recipes.

Makes about 4 cups

Bizcochitos

Come Christmastime, bakers throughout the Southwest make these crisp little anise-flavored cookies. They're traditionally cut into geometric shapes, stars, and other standard holiday shapes.

1 1/2 cups sugar

1 cup unsalted butter

2 eggs

1 1/2 teaspoons anise seed

1 teaspoon brandy

1 teaspoon pure vanilla extract

2 1/2 cups all-purpose flour

1 teaspoon baking powder

Pinch of salt

Cinnamon and sugar mixed together, for sprinkling over the cookies

In a food processor with the metal blade, cream together the sugar and butter. Pulse in the eggs, anise, brandy, and vanilla. Transfer the mixture to a mixing bowl.

In a separate bowl, sift together the flour, baking powder, and salt. Using your fingers, gradually work these dry ingredients into the creamed mixture to make a smooth, thick dough. Gather the dough into a ball, wrap in plastic wrap, and refrigerate for several hours.

Preheat the oven to 375 degrees F. Cut the dough into 4 pieces and roll them out one at a time on a lightly floured surface to a thickness of 1/4 inch. Cut the dough with cookie cutters, lightly sprinkle the shapes with cinnamon sugar, and place them on ungreased cookie sheets.

Bake until golden, 7 to 10 minutes. Cool on a wire rack, then store in an airtight container.

Makes 2 to 3 dozen, depending on size

57

Piñon Brittle

This is delicious broken over vanilla ice cream.

1 cup shelled piñones

2 cups granulated sugar

1 tablespoon butter, at room temperature

Spread the piñones in a 9-inch-square non-stick baking pan. Put the pan in a 450-degree F oven to toast the pine nuts for several minutes until very light golden (watch them carefully, since they darken quickly), then remove the pan from the oven and set aside.

Put the sugar in a heavy saucepan over very low heat and cook, stirring constantly until it melts completely, about 10 minutes. Stir in the butter and immediately pour the syrup over the piñones.

When the brittle has cooled and hardened, turn it out of the pan, cover with waxed paper or a kitchen towel, and hit it with a mallet or your fist to break it into irregular pieces. Store in an airtight container.

Makes about 1 pound

A sidewalk stall offers an appealingly casual array of candy brittles chockful of piñones, pumpkin seeds, and other nutmeats. To anyone who has traveled south of the border, such confections clearly reflect the Mexican influence on the cooking of the region.

Guacamole

When is a recipe not a recipe? Here's a good example. I always find that the best—and the most fun—way to make a good guacamole is to keep on tasting it as you mix. So, apart from the avocados themselves, take the quantities below as just basic guidelines, mixing the guacamole to your own liking.

Use the bumpy-skinned, Haas variety of avocados—*not* the smooth-skinned, larger variety.

Mix this up just before serving for the freshest flavor and to guard against discoloration. Serve with Tostaditas (see page 48) or as a garnish for almost any Southwestern main course you might cook up.

*2 large, fully ripe avocados,
halved, pitted, and peeled*

*1 medium tomato, cored, seeded,
and coarsely chopped*

*2 to 3 tablespoons fresh lime
or lemon juice*

*1 to 2 tablespoons finely chopped
canned green chiles*

1 to 2 tablespoons finely grated mild onion

Salt and freshly ground white pepper

In a mixing bowl, coarsely mash the avocados with a fork, leaving some chunks about $^1/_2$ inch in size.

Stir in the remaining ingredients to taste. Serve immediately.

Serves 4

Refries

As often as you see whole beans on the menu as a side dish, you'll find these luscious mashed beans, "refried" (a slight misnomer, since they've never been fried before) in a little bacon fat—or vegetable oil for vegetarians—and topped with cheddar and jack cheese.

*3 tablespoons bacon drippings
or vegetable oil*

4 cups cooked whole frijoles

$^1/_2$ cup shredded Cheddar cheese

$^1/_2$ cup shredded Monterey Jack cheese

In a large skillet, heat the drippings or oil over moderate heat. Add the beans and, as they cook, mash and stir them with a potato masher until they form a thick purée of coarsely mashed beans. When they're heated through and any liquid has evaporated, spoon them onto serving plates and immediately top them with the shredded cheeses.

Serves 6 to 8

SUPERSTARS OF CONTEMPORARY SOUTHWESTERN CUISINE

In the beginning was the taco, the enchilada, the relleno, the rice, and the beans. (And don't forget a side of guacamole.) Even as recently as the 1970s, any one of us would have been forgiven for scoffing at the use of the words *Southwestern* and *cuisine* in the same sentence.

But Southwestern cuisine is a very real force in today's American culinary scene. And its strength has grown like that of any great cuisine—out of humble roots. Take the greatest French *nouvelle cuisine:* its foundation is the rustic cooking of the provinces. The finest *alta cucina* of Italian cooking elevates the *cucina rustica* of humble homes. Why can't Southwestern cooking make the same transformation?

That's the very question enterprising young chefs of the region started to make in the 1980s. Their bold experiments—combining traditional ingredients and cooking vernacular with the refined sensibilities and far-reaching influences of the contemporary kitchen—have resulted in restaurants of national and international renown, restaurants with staying power.

While scores of chefs have successfully contributed to contemporary Southwestern cuisine, several names stand out—among them John Sedlar, Janos Wilder, Stephan Pyles, and Mark Miller, who share here a quartet of recipes that demonstrate just how far we've come since the combination plates of our childhoods.

John Sedlar

It's ironic that John Sedlar, the man generally credited with pioneering modern Southwestern cuisine, had no intention at all of cooking Southwestern food. Born near Santa Fe, of a Hispanic mother and an Anglo father, he started out cooking professionally there in 1971 at a restaurant that featured both local and French cuisines. He stuck resolutely to the latter and moved to Los Angeles in 1973, at the very beginnings of California's culinary flowering. Realizing eventually that he'd need a truly classical training to succeed in his chosen profession, he apprenticed himself in 1976 to L.A.'s renowned chef Jean Bertranou, founder of L'Ermitage. With the skills and artistry he acquired there, in 1980 Sedlar and partner Steve Garcia opened Saint Estephe, a tiny restaurant serving nouvelle cuisine in the coastal suburb of Manhattan Beach.

Over the next two years, Sedlar became increasingly aware of the resurgent interest in real American cooking. Late in 1982 he began to experiment with New Mexican red chiles and other ingredients of his homeland, incorporating them into his French-style dishes and offering those creations on a small "menu within a menu." Within a few months, more than three-quarters of the dishes ordered at Saint Estephe were from what Sedlar dubbed his "Modern Southwest Cuisine," and in the spring of 1983 the restaurant changed over almost completely to these innovative new recipes that combined French techniques with native New Mexican ingredients in an array of vivid, visually witty variations on traditional Southwestern dishes: red cabbage tacos filled with duck, green chile soufflés, steamed chile rellenos filled with mushroom purée and served with a garlic–goat cheese sauce. Accolades, both local and national, came quickly, and Sedlar's renown follows him and Garcia at their second restaurant, Bikini, in Santa Monica.

One of Sedlar's presentations that constantly excites comment is a caviar appetizer that mimics the faces of kachina dolls. Though elaborate looking and elegant, it's actually quite easy to make, and needn't cost that much if you use some of the excellent domestic caviars now widely available.

Kachina Mosaic of Caviars with Endive Feathers

This arrangement of caviars, chopped eggs, and onions gets its pattern from the faces of kachina dolls and kachina masks. It's surprising how closely its colors match the vivid paints actually used by the Indians in their folk art.

1 pound large Belgian endives, leaves separated

2 hard-boiled eggs

3 tablespoons American golden caviar (whitefish roe)

2 tablespoons finely chopped fresh parsley

3 tablespoons American sturgeon caviar

1 tablespoon salmon caviar

1 tablespoon finely chopped onion

Select about 2 dozen of the best endive leaves of roughly equal size (about 5 inches long). Set them aside.

Separate the yolks from the whites of the eggs. Finely chop both.

Draw a circle 7 inches in diameter on a sheet of paper. Following a photograph, or your own imagination, draw a kachina doll face in the circle. Place a 7-inch glass plate on top of the circle and use the circle and the doll face as your guide to assembling the kachina doll mosaic. Center the plate with the completed mosaic on top of a 12-inch serving plate; place a rim of endive leaves completely surrounding and radiating from the mosaic like a feather headdress.

Serves 4

Janos Wilder

One of the most extraordinary dining experiences in Tucson—or in any other Southwestern city, for that matter—can be found at Janos, which takes its name from owner-chef Janos Wilder.

Set in a historic nineteenth-century adobe residence that shares a spacious plaza with the city's art museum, Janos presents food of remarkably delicate flavor, arrayed with a simple, exuberant artistry. Everything reflects Wilder's far-ranging culinary experience: from his native Menlo Park, California, where he began cooking at a Magoo's Pizza Parlor at the age of 16; to Nashville; to Gold Hill, Colorado; to the solid European training he received at the respected La Réserve and Le Duberne in Bordeaux, France; to his home in Tucson, where Southwestern traditions and ingredients provide a never-ending source of inspiration.

Janos generously shares here a recipe that demonstrates the honest, classical simplicity and style of his cuisine:

Bay Scallop Salsa

Kernels from 1 ear sweet corn

1/2 large red onion, diced small

1 large tomato, diced medium

1/2 large red bell pepper, diced small

1/2 large green bell pepper, diced small

1/2 tablespoon finely chopped garlic

1/2 cup dry white wine

4 ounces fresh bay scallops

4 tablespoons cooked black beans

2 tablespoons butter at room temperature

Salt and freshly ground pepper

Chives for garnish

For the bay scallop salsa, combine the corn, onion, tomatoes, red and green bell peppers, garlic, and wine in a saucepan and simmer for 3 minutes. Add scallops and simmer an additional 2 minutes. Stir in beans. Remove from heat and whisk in butter until emulsified.

Divide salsa among 4 warm dinner plates and serve cabrilla on top of sauce. Crisscross 2 long chives over the top.

Serves 4

Grilled Baja Cabrilla with Bay Scallop Salsa

Cabrilla is a 7- to 40-pound sea bass fished in the Sea of Cortez, near Baja California. A meaty, clean-tasting fish, it is perfect for grilling and hearty enough to stand up to the hottest of Southwestern preparations.

The salsa provides an excellent contrast of sea and earth elements (bay scallops simmered with sweet corn, black beans, and chiles) that brings out the characteristic texture and flavor of the cabrilla.

4 thick cabrilla fillets (6 1/2 ounces each)

For grilling: a mixture of 1/2 cup olive oil, 1 tablespoon chopped garlic, and salt and pepper to taste

Salt and freshly ground pepper

Prepare gas or wood grill.

Lightly brush cabrilla with olive oil mixture and sprinkle with salt and pepper to taste. Grill until medium rare, turning once, about 4 minutes per side. To form grill marks, rotate fillets 90 degrees after 2 minutes on first side, then continue cooking.

© Lois Ellen Frank

Stephan Pyles

Contemporary Southwestern cooking of a superior kind may be found at Dallas's Routh Street Cafe and its smaller sibling, Baby Routh—both brainchildren of owner-chef Stephan Pyles. A native Texan, Pyles credits his cuisine first to three strong influences that go back to his childhood and to his family's Truck-Stop Cafe: Tex-Mex cooking, with its Southwestern vernacular of chiles, tamales, and enchiladas; Southern foods, from barbecue to catfish, to fried chicken; and the down-home elegance of Creole and Cajun kitchens.

Grafted onto that background is the experience Pyles gained—after finishing a college degree in music—by working in France with such masters as Alain Chapel, Roger Verge, Michel Guerard, and the Troisgros brothers. "I use classic techniques," he says, "in combination with indigenous products to prepare sophisticated dishes with a Southwest flair."

This recipe is a cunning cross between a steamed tamale and a French-style quiche.

FOODS

Roast Garlic Custard

1 tablespoon olive oil

6 large cloves garlic, peeled

2 cups heavy cream

4 egg yolks

1 whole egg

Salt to taste (about 3/4 teaspoon)

Freshly ground white pepper to taste

Preheat the oven to 300 degrees F. Heat the olive oil in a small roasting pan and toss in the garlic. Place pan in oven and roast garlic until golden brown, about 15 minutes.

Place roasted garlic in a saucepan with cream and bring to a boil. Place in blender and purée garlic completely, about 1 minute.

In a mixing bowl, beat whole egg and yolks together, then drizzle in the garlic-cream mixture while stirring. Season with salt and white pepper. Set aside.

Serves 8 to 10

Tamale Tart with Roast Garlic Custard and Gulf Coast Crabmeat

Roast Garlic Custard

1 1/4 cups masa harina

3/4 cup yellow cornmeal

2 teaspoons salt

1/4 teaspoon cayenne

2 teaspoons cumin

10 tablespoons shortening

2 tablespoons red bell pepper purée

2 tablespoons ancho chile purée

2 tablespoons olive oil

4 tablespoons diced onion

10 ounces Gulf Coast lump crabmeat, carefully picked over

4 tablespoons diced red tomatoes

4 tablespoons diced yellow tomatoes

2 tablespoons cilantro

2 teaspoons diced serrano chiles

1 teaspoon lime juice

Salt to taste

Make Roast Garlic Custard and set aside at room temperature while preparing tart.

Combine masa harina, cornmeal, salt, cayenne, and cumin and set aside. In a mixing bowl, whip the shortening with hand mixer until light and fluffy. Gradually add dry ingredients and continue to whip until well blended and smooth. Whip in red pepper and ancho purées and form into a ball.

Pat the dough into a 9-inch false-bottom tart pan and press to flatten on bottom and up sides.

Fill with the roast garlic custard mix and cover tart pan completely with plastic wrap.

Place in bamboo steamer set over boiling water and steam for 25 to 30 minutes.

When tart is cooked, heat the olive oil in a medium sauté pan until lightly smoking. Add the onion and saute for 1 minute. Add crabmeat, tomatoes, cilantro, serranos, and lime juice. Cook until warmed through, about 2 minutes. Place on top of tart and slice into pieces.

Mark Miller

Hands down, Santa Fe's hottest restaurant is Coyote Cafe, the latest chapter—and an enduring one—in the international culinary odyssey of chef Mark Miller. Born in New England to a French-Canadian family, Miller first encountered spicy cooking through a family friend from Guadalajara. He went on to study, and later teach, anthropology at U.C. Berkeley, where he also cooked for fun, as well as beginning a gourmet newsletter and working for Williams-Sonoma. Eventually, he was offered a job in the kitchen at Alice Waters's legendary Chez Panisse, where he worked for three and a half years, finally leaving to open the very successful Fourth Street Grill in 1979.

There, Miller began to play with the spicy foods he encountered and loved on his frequent travels to the Southwest as well as Central America, North Africa, and Southeast Asia. He concentrated on spicy North American cuisines with his second Berkeley restaurant, the Santa Fe Bar and Grill—named not just for the New Mexican capital but for the establishment's actual site, once a depot of the Santa Fe Railroad.

The beauty, the setting, and the foods of Santa Fe had long haunted Miller, and he moved there in 1985, opening Coyote Cafe two years later. A cavernous yet intimate space vividly alive with folk art animals, the restaurant presents bold new Southwestern dishes—from lobster enchiladas to braised duck with posole, red chile risotto clams to venison chile—that reflect the owner-chef's strong background in anthropology, his many travels, and most of all his love of cooking.

And some of Miller's Southwestern recipes still bear the mark of his earliest culinary experiences, as this recipe from Coyote vividly demonstrates:

Green Chile and Oyster Chowder

"Once again," says Miller, "this recipe reflects my Northeastern background, where homemade chowders made from onions, milk, potatoes, and clams were ever present. This is a Southwestern adaptation of one of my favorites. The ingredients are precooked and added at the last minute so they retain their flavor and identity. Use whole large oysters, as smaller ones will dry out and not have the plump, rich center that you want. Shucked oysters are likely to be freshest at the local fish market; fresh scallops can be used as an alternative. In this soup you do not want any hint of smokiness, so the chiles are blistered in hot oil, not roasted or grilled. For a richer chowder, use heavy cream instead of half-and-half."

1 pound red potatoes, cut into 1/2-inch dice

1 medium onion, finely chopped

2 1/2 cups fish stock (or clam juice)

1 bay leaf

1/2 pound fresh green chiles

2 cups peanut oil

1/2 cup fresh corn kernels

16 shucked oysters in their liquor

1 large sweet red pepper, roasted, peeled, and cut into 1/2-inch dice

2 cups half-and-half

salt to taste

1 tablespoon butter

1 teaspoon fresh marjoram, chopped

Gently boil the potatoes for about 4 minutes in salted water, rinse, and cool. Cook the onion with 1 cup of stock and the bay leaf over low heat for 15 to 20 minutes, until cooked through, but not browned. Discard the bay leaf and cool. Fry the green chiles in the oil for about 4 or 5 minutes until the skin is blistered, but not blackened. Skin the chiles, remove seeds, and cut into 1/2-inch dice. Steam the corn in 1/4 cup water in a covered pan for 2 minutes until tender.

In a large pan, combine the oysters with their liquor, the remaining stock, and the green chiles. Heat for 2 minutes, then add the potatoes, onion, and red pepper, and bring to a boil. Add the half-and-half, keeping the mixture below a boil to keep the half-and-half from separating. Add salt, corn, and butter. Pour into soup bowls and garnish with the marjoram.

Serves 4

FOODS

WINES OF THE SOUTHWEST

West Coast wineries have been getting so much attention in recent years that they've all but eclipsed the fact that there's also a burgeoning wine industry in the Southwest.

Wine from the desert? It sounds like some biblical miracle. But grown at high desert elevations—between 2,500 and 5,000 feet above sea level—grapes enjoy a more moderate climate that, along with the rich soil, promotes the development of varietal character essential to making quality wines. Add the ever-more-sophisticated techniques developed by wine science, and you have the conditions that have given rise to some two dozen quality vineyards in New Mexico and Arizona, along with a handful of boutique wineries in Colorado and Texas.

To dare to generalize in a subject area that usually dwells on subtleties, one could say that the climate produces more robust-tasting grapes for wines whose power more than compensates for any lack of finesse they might exhibit. Which makes them, in their own way, an excellent match for the cuisine of the Southwest.

New vineyards with great wines pop up all the time. And a number of vineyards have already proven themselves, offering an excellent opportunity for you to begin your acquaintance with the wines of the Southwest. Here are a few recommendations:

Arizona

Sonoita Vineyards Perhaps the most respected Southwestern vineyard, this winery near Tucson has already produced remarkable Cabernet Sauvignon, Chenin Blanc, and Fume Blanc.
R.W. Webb Winery Near Tucson, this young winery is already producing fine examples of Cabernet Sauvignon, Chenin Blanc, and French Colombard.

New Mexico

La Chiripada Winery The excellent Reserve Riesling from this winery between Santa Fe and Taos has won plaudits from many connoisseurs, including Steve Garcia of Saint Estephe restaurant. Also recommended: a delicate blush wine called Vino Sonrojo, and their robust Rojo Grande.
St. Clair Vineyards This young winery near Las Cruces in the southern part of the state has already made a mark with both a good, crisp Sauvignon Blanc and a light, sweet, and spicy dessert wine made from the Muscat Canelli grape. Keep an eye on their emerging Chardonnay and Cabernet Sauvignon.
Blue Teal Vineyards Near Lordsburg in western New Mexico, Blue Teal is noted for its fresh-tasting Riesling and white Zinfandel.

Texas

Fall Creek Vineyards On the Colorado River in central Texas, Fall Creek is well known for light, drinkable Chenin Blanc and Emerald Riesling, as well as their Carnelian—a red wine reminiscent of Beaujolais. Also recommended: Sauvignon Blanc, Semillon, Chardonnay, and Cabernet Sauvignon.
Llano Estacado Winery In northwestern Texas's Lubbock County, this winery specializes in good, crisp Chardonnay, Riesling, and Chenin Blanc. Also notable: Cabernet Sauvignon and a Cabernet rose.
Pheasant Ridge Winery This Lubbock County vineyard has won praise for its Cabernet Sauvignon, Barbara, Chardonnay, and Sauvignon and Chenin Blancs.

SOUTHWESTERN CRAFTS & COLLECTIBLES

Throughout his life, Santa Fe transplant Alexander Girard—a renowned collector of international folk art—had thought of his collection, which includes numerous Southwestern objects, as a toy *collection. But when his Girard Foundation signed an agreement with the Museum of International Folk Art (MOIFA) donating some 106,000 objects collected by Girard to the state of New Mexico, one of the museum's stipulations was that the word* toy *be dropped from the collection's official name.*

While in no way belittling the magnitude of Girard's achievement or his own deep love and respect for the objects he collected and their makers, the MOIFA's viewpoint suggests the ever-growing seriousness with which the crafts of the Southwest have come to be regarded. To be sure, some collectors have always found beauty and meaning in the works of the region's Native American and Hispanic artisans, but past generations for the most part, evidence suggests, regarded the indigenous crafts at best as charming toys and lovely objects.

But with the rediscovery of the Southwest in recent decades, we've begun to appreciate more fully the true meanings behind these works of art and the roles they play in the lives of the people who make them. We've learned more about the complex spirit world represented by the Hopi kachinas, the nature-inspired designs of the Navajo blanket, the sublime beauty vested in everyday objects by the San Ildefonso potters, and the interplay of witty self-expression and heartfelt devotion exhibited by the creations of a santero.

And in such deeper insights, we may well achieve an understanding that transcends the culture of the Southwest alone. As Alexander Girard wrote in his foreword to Multiple Visions: A Common Bond, *the exhibition catalog for his collection,* "Folk Art tells us there are no 'foreigners.' The colors vary, their languages vary, but their spirits and aspirations are interwoven into one incredibly rich humanity."

In recent years, respect for native artifacts of the Southwest has grown tremendously among collectors worldwide, with prices for antique pieces like the 1880s Navajo blanket on page 70 or authentic Hopi kachinas dating from as recently as the early half of the twentieth century (left) rocketing to many hundreds, thousands, even tens of thousands of dollars. But the authentic work of more contemporary craftspersons—from blankets to kachinas to pottery, along with a wealth of other artforms—is still within reach of most collectors' budgets. Blankets and rugs bring the Southwest vividly into any home.

A TALE OF THREE COLLECTIONS

The world's appreciation of Southwestern folk art and culture has been vastly enriched by three outstanding collections—those of Dwight and Maie Heard, Millicent Rogers, and Alexander and Susan Girard—whose bequests to the public make it possible today for everyone to study and enjoy the fruits of their private labors.

The Heard Museum

In 1894, Chicago businessman Dwight Heard contracted a lung ailment that led his doctors to suggest a move to warmer, drier climes. After a year of travel in the Southwest, he and his wife, Maie, decided to settle in the young and growing town of Phoenix, where over the next three decades he became a prominent real estate developer, rancher, and newspaper publisher.

Soon after they settled, the couple began to collect native artifacts of the region, which they eventually displayed to beautiful effect in their showplace home built in 1903, which they called Casa Blanca. In 1926, they bought a site in Phoenix containing Hohokam Indian ruins, and hired an amateur archaeologist to excavate the ruins and open them to public viewing.

Their collection became so extensive that their daughter-in-law Winifred suggested it be turned into a public museum. A gracious Spanish Colonial-style building was raised on the grounds of Casa Blanca, and the Heard Museum officially opened in the summer of 1929, just a few months after Dwight Heard's sudden death from a heart attack. For the next twenty-two years, Maie Heard continued to foster the legacy she had begun with her husband, actively supporting the museum's educational work and the growth of its collection of artifacts.

Today, the Heard stands as an outstanding resource of native artifacts and a superb example of contemporary museum design. Of particular note is its exhibit "Native Peoples of the Southwest," which presents textiles, ceramics, basketry, and other artifacts within a comprehensive survey of the region's tribes and its varied geography. One particular pleasure is a room displaying over five hundred kachina dolls collected by the Fred Harvey Company and Arizona senator Barry Goldwater—shelf after shelf of colorful, intricately detailed effigies of the Hopi spirit world. What's more, the museum frequently hosts native artists-in-residence, offering a close-up look at the creation of modern masterworks of Southwestern culture.

The Millicent Rogers Museum

"You'll get an amazing feeling of déjà vu," a friend warned me before my first visit to the Millicent Rogers Museum, just outside of Taos. "You'll look at all the objects on display and you'll swear you've seen them before. Then it'll dawn on you that you have—in every book you've ever seen on Native American arts."

The collection assembled by Millicent Rogers is indeed definitive—some of the finest examples anywhere of Southwestern arts and artifacts. Heiress to the Standard Oil fortune, society beauty Rogers first visited Taos in the early 1940s and moved there in 1947. Falling in love with the area, its thriving arts scene, and its native culture, she began to apply her finely honed aesthetic sensibilities to the acquisition of pieces produced by the region's tribes. After her death, family members founded the museum in 1953, opening it to the public three years later.

Small and select, the Millicent Rogers Museum centers on its namesake's superb collections of kachina dolls, Navajo and Pueblo jewelry, Navajo textiles, Pueblo pottery, Southwestern basketry, and other artifacts. More recent acquisitions by the museum foundation are also on display, including works by famed San Ildefonso potter Maria Martinez, and secular and religious artifacts reflecting the Southwest's Hispanic heritage.

Conceived, designed, and donated by collector Alexander Girard, the multicultural exhibition known as Multiple Visions is the showpiece of Santa Fe's Museum of International Folk Art. The Girard wing includes case after case of often surprisingly moving tableaux—such as the wake scene of painted earthenware figures shown below, created around 1960 by the Aguilar family of Oaxaca, Mexico.

The Girard Collection

Since the 1930s, Italian-born architect and interior designer Alexander Girard and his wife Susan have avidly—or, to be even more accurate, obsessively—collected folk art from around the world. With their move to Santa Fe in 1953, after Alexander had successfully launched his American career in the Detroit area, the Girard collection continued to grow, becoming the largest of its kind in the world. In 1978, the couple donated that collection, numbering some 106,000 individual objects, to Santa Fe's Museum of International Folk Art, with the provision that they be housed in their own separate exhibition wing, which was completed in 1980.

In 1982, the Alexander Girard–conceived exhibition *Multiple Visions* opened to the public in that wing, and it stands as a lasting tribute to his brilliance as both a designer and a collector. In a vast hall, tens of thousands of pieces from the Girard Collection are arranged in displays, vignettes, and dioramas that emphasize the commonality of human experience.

Naturally enough, Southwestern folk arts enjoy a significant presence here, but they are seen in contexts that foster an enlightened world view. Navajo pictorial rugs portraying the American flag fly above a miniature Italian villa scene. Southwestern *santos* share a case with Italian *putti*, Mexican *diablos*, Scandinavian angels, and several dozen other figures in a lively international display called "Heaven and Hell." Kachina-like *kosharis* representing Pueblo ritual clowns appear near figurines from India, Morocco, Mexico, and elsewhere. At every turn, the eye encounters more juxtapositions.

In his foreword to the exhibition catalog for *Multiple Visions*, Girard quoted a favorite old Italian proverb: *"Tutto il mondo è paese"*—"The whole world is hometown." In the Girard Collection, that proverb finds its fullest, most eloquent expression.

NAVAJO WEAVINGS: RECENT EXPRESSIONS OF AN ANCIENT ART

Until just over three hundred years ago, the people now acclaimed as the preeminent weavers of the Southwest did not know how to weave. While they'd been coming to the region since around A.D. 1000, the nomadic Navajo tribe began to settle there in significant numbers only in the very early sixteenth century, learning from the Pueblos how to farm the land and raise sheep. And the women of such Pueblo tribes as the Tewa also gradually passed along to their Navajo sisters the skill of working the loom. Like the Pueblos, they began by producing simply striped designs in earth tones: brown, black, gray, and white.

As the years passed, the Navajo weavers began to vary the traditional designs, introducing more dynamic geometric forms and patterns; different villages and regions developed their own signature styles. Spanish settlers introduced dyes for the vibrant fabric colors of indigo and red; native plants were probed to yield an enhanced palette of subtler shades: yellows, greens, rusts, and so on. By the late nineteenth century, prespun wools and packaged dyes expanded the Navajo palette even further.

Today, Navajo weaving—whether a century-old historical blanket or a vivid contemporary rug by a leading craftsperson—is prized for both its artistry and its quality. Both practical and beautiful, it is equally at home on the living-room floor or wall.

A Navajo child's blanket dating from the 1880s demonstrates the intricate and carefully controlled symmetrical design of this Native American artform.

Over time, and with the advent of a wider palette of dyes and even more sophisticated weaving techniques, Navajo textiles have become increasingly varied and complex, in some cases with different regions noted for particular kinds of designs. A storm pattern rug created in the 1970s (near right), depicting abstractions of meteorological phenomena, is typical of weavings from the area of Tuba City, Arizona. The bold patterns and bright colors of a rug made during the 1960s (second right) help to identify it as a weaving of the Red Mesa style. The elongated forms of ceremonial figures on a horizontal rug woven during the 1970s (opposite) typify the style known as Ye'ii.

A Navajo Weaving Style Glossary

To help you identify Navajo weavings and choose the ones that best suit your taste, here's a brief survey of some characteristic styles:

© Henry Kahn/Courtesy of The Native American Art Gallery

Chinle

From the area of Canyon de Chelly, broadly striped, borderless rugs in solid vegetable colors, elaborated with geometric squash blossom designs.

Crystal

Subtle vegetable-dye colors—browns, greens, yellows, grays—combine in wavy bands or stripes, in the artisanry of this weaving center north of Window Rock in New Mexico.

Ganado

Geometric patterns typified by a prevalent deep, warm red color—known as "Ganado red"—complemented by black, gray, and white.

Sand Paintings

Designs inspired by the sand paintings made as a part of traditional Navajo religious ceremonies; some small part of the design is changed to avoid sacrilege.

Storm Pattern

Rugs featuring geometric abstractions of lightning, storm clouds, and water, with a large central square and smaller boxes at the corners. Prevalent in the Tuba City, Arizona, area.

© Henry Kahn/Courtesy of The Native American Art Gallery

Teec Nos Pos / Red Mesa

A region near Shiprock in northern New Mexico, near the Four Corners, known for its patterns of bold geometric shapes outlined in brightly contrasting colors. The rugs' wide borders often have a large, T-shaped design.

Two Grey Hills

The name of a trading post at Toadlena, New Mexico, noted for its finely woven rugs in simple patterns and subtle colors.

Wide Ruins

From the southeastern corner of the Navajo reservation, subdued geometric flourishes within a finely weaved striped pattern, colored with subtle earth-toned vegetable dyes.

Ye'ii

Horizontal weavings in which the traditional stripes are replaced by elongated ceremonial human or godlike figures.

Originally woven to be worn, a Navajo serape dating from the 1870s becomes a modern showpiece well worthy of decorative display and aesthetic appreciation (opposite). Careful attention to how it is hung or where it might be placed on the floor, its exposure to light, heat and humidity, and how it is cleaned, will ensure that the magnificent textile will last for many decades, even centuries, to come.

80

Caring for Navajo Textiles

While Navajo textiles, both antique and contemporary, are created primarily for practical use as garments, wall decorations, or floor rugs, their value as beautiful objects, historical artifacts, and coveted collectibles raises serious concerns over how best to take care of them in the home. These few guidelines will help you keep your textiles in peak condition for as long as possible.

Display

• Use only textiles of the heaviest weave as floor rugs.

• Do not put floor rugs in heavily trafficked areas, such as halls or doorways.

• To minimize wear, cushion floor rugs with a thick underpad, and use furniture coasters if necessary.

• Display lighter-textured weavings as wall decorations.

• To help conserve their shape, hang weavings with their warps vertical, their wefts horizontal, and the finishing end on top.

• Use a Velcro-style hanging system, which will not distort the weaving the way rods, rings, or hooks do.

• Hanging in a Plexiglass box will help protect weavings from airborne dirt.

Light, Temperature, and Humidity

• To slow down the fading that naturally occurs with exposure to light, keep weavings away from direct sunlight and display them in low-light areas of the home.

• Don't shine spotlights directly on weavings.

• To minimize exposure to harmful ultraviolet light, you might consider shielding windows and illumination sources with UV filters.

• Try to maintain a humidity neither too high (which could lead to distortion of a weaving's shape and promotes mildew) nor too low (which dries out the fabric, making it brittle).

• Avoid high temperatures (which dry out fabrics under low humidity and promote mildew and rot at high humidity) and temperature fluctuations (which distress the weavings).

• Don't display textiles near heating or air-conditioning vents, or in kitchens.

Cleaning and Pest Control

• Clean all but the most fragile textiles by vacuuming them monthly, front and back, using a nozzle attachment that allows you to follow your progress close up and in detail.

• Regularly and thoroughly vacuum all areas near the rug to eliminate any chance of areas such as baseboards harboring insects or their larvae: Navajo rugs are easily destroyed by moths and carpet beetles.

• Closely inspect rugs for signs of infestation: small holes, droppings, larvae, or the insects themselves. If necessary, have the textiles professionally fumigated.

• Immediately and thoroughly blot up—without rubbing—any spills from rugs.

• In case of heavily soiled rugs, have them custom dry-cleaned by hand.

*O our Mother the
Earth, O our Father
the Sky,
Your children are we,
and with tired backs
We bring you the
gifts that you love.
Then weave for us
a garment of
brightness;
May the warp be
the white light of
morning,
May the weft be the
red light of evening,
May the fringes be
the falling rain,
May the border
be the standing
rainbow.
Thus weave for us
a garment of
brightness
That we may walk
fittingly where the
birds sing,
That we may walk
fittingly where the
grass is green,
O our Mother the
Earth, O our Father
the Sky.*

   *—Tewa Song
   of the Loom*

81

MODERN MASTERS OF PUEBLO POTTERY

This century's growing interest in Southwestern arts has had perhaps its most dramatic effect on the craft of pottery making among the Pueblo peoples. In recent decades, Pueblo potters have won international acclaim, signing their names for eternity to works firmly rooted in a tradition dating back some two thousand years to craftspeople whose efforts will remain forever anonymous.

Working without a wheel, as their forebears did, the potters of today build up their pots in spiraling coils, smoothing them to an elegant, classic symmetry and then decorating them with their own interpretations of traditional motifs. Yet within the confines of tradition, these potters do indeed achieve distinctively personal, freshly modern artistic expressions. Here are profiles of some of the masters.

Maria Martinez of San Ildefonso

Any list of noteworthy potters inevitably must begin with Maria, who, working with her husband Julian and later with her daughter-in-law Santana and her son Popovi Da, perfected the famous black-on-black style of pottery, in which matte-black geometric and nature-inspired designs march around a glossy black finish.

Margaret and Luther Gutierrez of Santa Clara

Noted for richly toned polychrome pottery in both very simple and elaborate shapes, elegantly decorated with animal, human, and geometric figures done in brown, black, and white.

Lucy Lewis of Acoma

Lucy's name comes a close second to Maria's, with a reputation well earned through polychrome pots with geometric and animal designs inspired by decorations from the prehistoric Mimbres pottery.

The Nampeyo Family

Descendants of Nampeyo, a Hopi woman born around 1860, still practice the prehistoric pottery styles she and her husband Lesou, an archaeological crew member, were instrumental in reviving. The low-shouldered pots are decorated in intricate designs of black and red set against a cream-colored background.

Sarafina Tafoya of Santa Clara

Descendents of the late Sarafina Tafoya, including her daughters Margaret and Christina and many granddaughters, make solid, simply shaped, brightly polished black pots, many of them decorated with ancient good-luck symbols—particularly a simple bear's-paw design.

As a little girl I used to watch my grandmother [Serafina Tafoya] and I thought someday I was going to be put in the Potter's Hands, which is God. I dedicated myself and my precious hands to the Lord to do this pottery. I ask the Lord to help me as I grow older to help me show my talent to the world as an individual.

I know the Lord has done something wonderful for me and it was His Will for me to have this talent. It is not a hobby; it is my living. And I have been doing this all by myself; I have no one to help me, only God. And today I thank Him. He is the Potter. He molds my life and I mold the potteries.

*—Teresita Naranjo,
quoted in*
Seven Families in
Pueblo Pottery

The basic coil method by which most South-western-style pottery is formed can yield vessels in a surprising variety of shapes and sizes that fulfill many different functions, including storage, cooking, serving, and pouring.

84

MAKING A SOUTH-WESTERN-STYLE POT

Most Southwestern Native American pottery is made by the ancient coil method—a technique home potters, whether novices or experienced, can follow with relative ease to make a very simple, traditional-style vessel suitable for display. The measurements provided are for a 6-inch-diameter pot. To make one larger or smaller, adjust amounts accordingly.

Materials Needed

4 pounds white, tan, or reddish brown clay

Scraping tool (old pottery pieces, smooth pebbles, table knife, cake-decorating implement, or professional potter's tool)

Red or brown poster paints, professional potters' paints and brush, or mesquite pitch (see step 6)

Directions

1. Roll firm, but moist and malleable pottery clay into ropes a foot long or more and $^1/_2$ to 1 inch in diameter, depending on the size of pot you will be making. For a 6-inch-diameter pot, you'll need about ten 2-foot lengths.

2. Starting at what will be the center of the pot's base, begin to coil the clay ropes, first forming a circular, flat base, and then gradually building the coil up and out from the rim of the base to form walls for the pot. As you add a new length of clay, firmly pinch its end together with that of the preceding length to secure them.

3. As the walls of the pot build up, gradually make their circumference narrower, ending in an opening about as wide as the base of the pot.

4. Using potters' scraping tools or other gently curved implements, gradually smooth the walls of the pot inside and out. Moisten and wipe the surfaces with your hands and a cloth to help achieve an even smoother finish.

5. Let the pot dry outdoors or at warm room temperature. If you have a pottery kiln, fire the dried pot, following time and temperatures appropriate for the clay you've used, or follow instructions, if appropriate for that particular clay, for baking in a kitchen oven. Alternatively, just let the pot air-dry completely.

6. If you're making an air-dried pot, use black or reddish brown poster paints to decorate the pot with Southwestern-style designs—perhaps inspired by some of the photographs in this book, or taken from your own imagination. For a kiln- or oven-fired pot, use professional pottery paints for the designs. Or, to be most authentic, gather the shiny black pitch found on the bark of mesquite trees; dissolve it in boiling water, then continue boiling until it reduces to the consistency of light cream; then use this concentrate to paint the design on the already-fired pot, heating the pot for about fifteen minutes in a home oven at the hottest temperature to set the color.

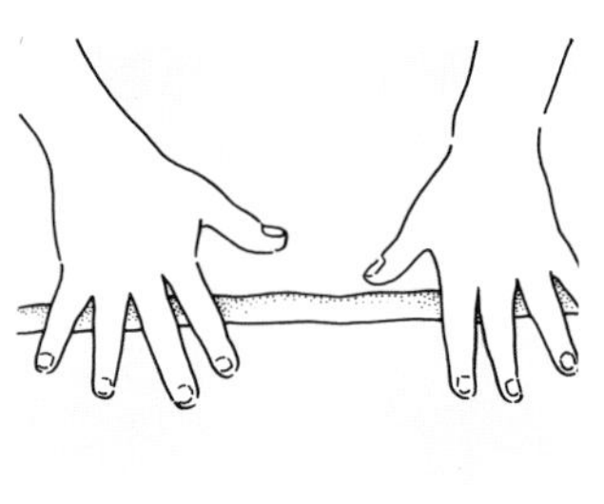

1

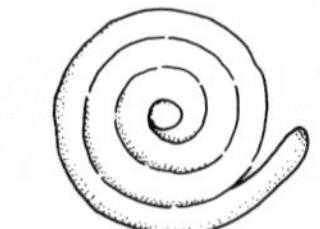

2

2

3

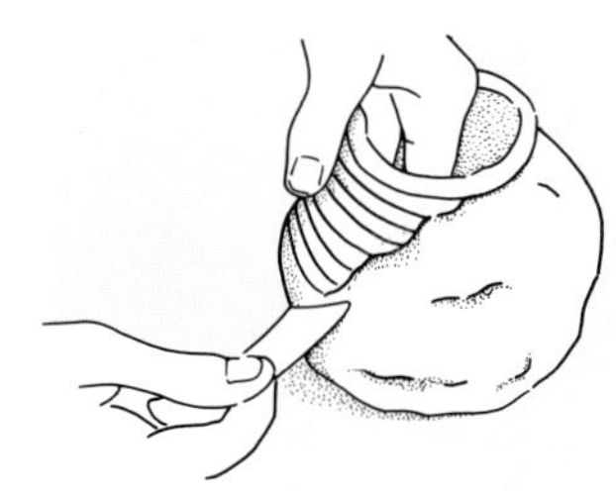

4

KACHINAS: EFFIGIES OF THE SPIRIT WORLD

© Joseph Saita/Courtesy of The Native American Art Gallery

Kachinas are magic to the children—and the adults—of the Hopi. In the native religion, kachinas represent the spirit realm, with every aspect of the physical world we experience having its corresponding kachina. While males of the tribe are inducted into the rituals of the kachina dance, portraying these spirits in life-sized form, female children are instructed in the cult of the kachina through gifts of carved and painted wooden figures—called *tihus*—that represent the various spirits and embody their powers. These prized possessions are hung from beams or placed safely on shelves to confer their blessings.

For more than a century and a half, outsiders have been collecting these figures—now commonly referred to in English as kachina dolls. While the production of kachina dolls has taken on a commercial aspect, many native carvers still strive for a high level of artistic achievement worthy of the *tihus's* exalted status, creating figures that, within the pueblo, continue to be invested with the same level of power they have always possessed. Representations have evolved over time and under the influence of market demand, with contemporary kachinas often appearing in more dynamic movements than the static-looking figures of the past.

So popular are kachinas today that members of other tribes have begun to participate in the Hopis' success. Since the 1970s, a number of Navajo artisans have been carving Hopi-style dolls— generally larger, less authentic-looking figures fashioned from heavier pine or other woods. While these dolls certainly have their own appeal, they should not in any way be taken as true kachinas, which can only be carved by the Hopis, most of whom live on or near one of twelve Hopi reservations.

Some Common and Less Common Kachinas

Part of the pleasure of collecting kachina dolls comes in deciding just which kinds you want to acquire of the three hundred or more deities represented by the dolls. You could aim for a comprehensive collection, concentrate on the works of one contemporary carver, or select one or more kind of doll, acquiring different interpretations of kachinas by a wide range of artists.

To start you on your way, here are a few suggestions of some appealing or unusual kachinas and the physical traits—representing actual kachinas from pueblo ceremonies—by which they are generally recognized:

Angwusnasomtaka (Crow Mother)

Recognized by the black crow's wings on either side of its head, this kachina—considered by some to be the mother of all kachinas—carries a bundle of yucca twigs with which children are whipped as part of their initiation into the kachina cult.

Eototo (Kachina Chief)

This father figure of all kachinas rules the seasons. Very simply carved and decorated, he is almost entirely white, with a rounded, ghostlike head.

Ka-e Kachina (Corn Dancer)

Ears of corn are depicted on the mask of this figure, whose dance helps the corn crop.

A very high level of artistry goes into the depiction of particular kachinas. A group of Hopi figures (opposite) dating from the 1940s and 1950s includes, from the left, a star kachina, a wolf, a rooster, and a Navajo clown. Fine feathers single out another kachina (left) as a kwahu, or eagle.

Koshari (Glutton)

While not a true kachina, this clown figure represents comic relief from the more serious Hopi ceremonies. Recognized by his black and white stripes, he is most often depicted in scenes of gluttony, most commonly gorging on watermelon.

Kwahu (Eagle)

A representation of the eagle's wings cover the arms of this popular kachina, whose dance encourages the growth of the eagle population.

A furry head and ferocious fangs typify a kweo or wolf kachina (right). Fashioned by contemporary Hopi artist A. Dennis, a patung or squash kachina (opposite) is readily identified by its green-painted body, gourdlike head, and hand-held blossoms.

Kweo (Wolf)

Fur covers the head of this kachina with its fierce-looking jaws—sometimes elaborated by a lolling tongue. The figure often carries a stick to represent the trees behind which the wolf hides while stalking deer or sheep.

Mongwa Wuhti (Great Horned Owl)

A dramatic mask resembling the owl's face characterizes this frequently carved kachina.

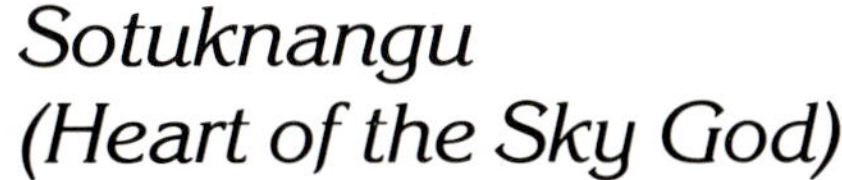

Sotuknangu (Heart of the Sky God)

A peaked hat on this kachina represents soaring thunderhead clouds, and the assembly of expandable crossed sticks he carries signifies lightning bolts.

Toho (Mountain Lion)

This brown-skinned figure resembles a mountain lion, complete with tail.

Toson Koyemsi (Sweet Cornmeal Tasting Mudhead)

A rounded mudhead mask with circular eyes and mouth and globular ears characterize this figure, which tastes and judges the sweetness of cornmeal that little girls grind to appease ogre kachinas.

Tsil (Chile)

A short kilt and a large-eyed mask topped by red chiles characterize this figure, which traditionally races against village men during springtime dances; if an opponent loses, the chiles are stuffed into his mouth.

Wiharu (White Ogre)

With popping eyes and fierce-looking white jaws, this disciplinary kachina is one of a group that scare children and teach them important lessons about communal, tribal living. Also recognized by the saw and the bow and arrows it carries.

Patung (Squash)

A green-and-black-striped, squash-shaped head, and a similarly painted body are the easy tip-off to this popular plant kachina, which also carries bright yellow squash blossoms in its hands and sometimes wears one as a hat.

Siyangephoya (Left-Handed Hunter)

As its name suggests, this hunter kachina looks awkward, holding its bow atypically in its right hand and drawing arrows with its left. It often has a garish, fiercely humorous expression.

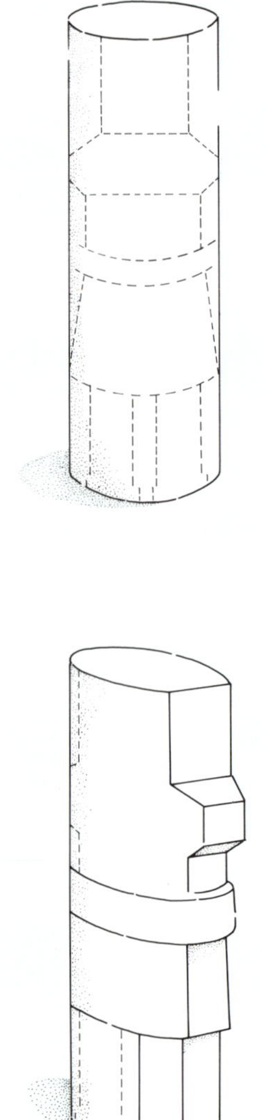

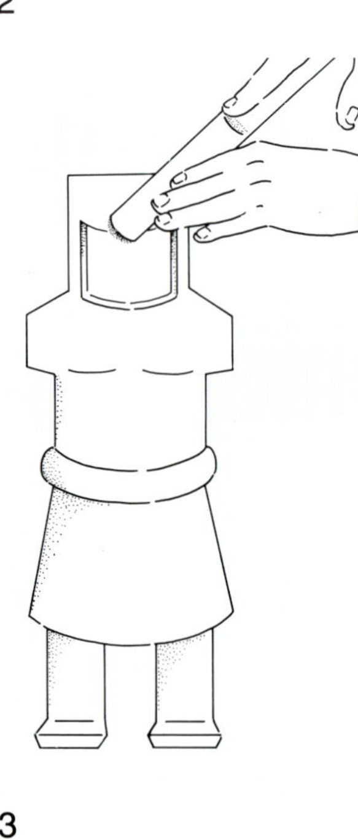

CARVING A KACHINA

A high-quality, elaborate kachina figure can take its artist several hundred hours of closely detailed work. Here are the basic steps involved in the process:

1. Choosing the wood. Cottonwood root has just the right texture and density for a kachina that carves fairly easily but still feels substantial and holds up to handling. For most standard-sized dolls, a straight, knot-free piece of root up to 1 foot long and 6 inches in diameter is selected.

2. Blocking out the figure. Shallow saw cuts are made at various levels around the root's circumference to block out the head, the ruff or neck, the torso and kilt, the legs and the feet.

3. Carving the figure. Using one or more small knives and files, the artist carves away the wood to shape the head and neck, torso and legs.

4. Carving the arms. In most cases, the arms are carved from thinner pieces of cottonwood root and glued to the main figure.

5. Sanding and priming. After final fine-detail carving, the kachina is sanded to a smooth finish and given a primer coat of paint.

6. Painting and finishing. Using fine brushes and acrylic paint, the artist paints the kachina in his or her interpretation of traditional patterns. Additional embellishments such as ceremonial rattles, feathers, fur, or strips of leather are also added at this time. The kachina is attached to a cross section of root—usually signed on its bottom by the artist—that serves as its base.

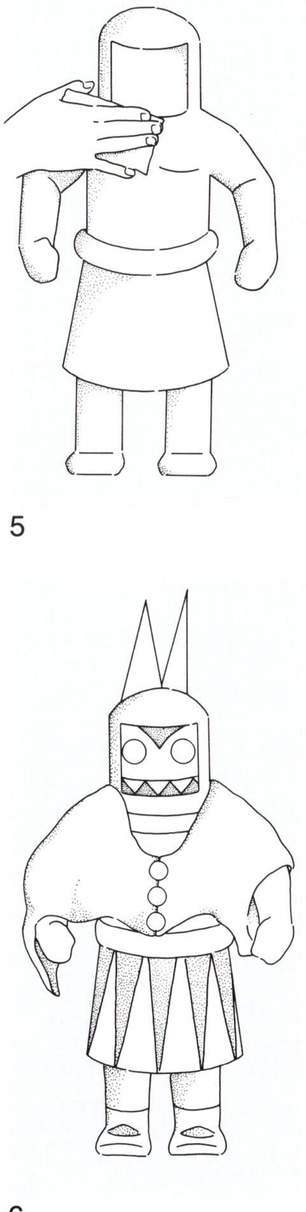

5

6

SAINTS AND BEASTS CARVED IN WOOD

Perhaps the most popular of all con-temporary Southwestern crafts, New Mexican wood carvings appeal to us because they show—more than any other indigenous artform—the hands of their makers. As the eye follows their contours, one can almost imagine the artisan at work, feeling the deft move-ments as he blocks out, carves, sands, and paints, discovering the image hid-den in a piece of cottonwood or pine.

The local wood carving tradition dates back some three hundred years, to early Spanish missionaries who brought with them handwrought wooden religious images. The art of making such saintly figures, or *santos*, flourished from the late eighteenth to mid-nineteenth centuries, as folk crafts-men known as *santeros* produced a wealth of religious figures for display in both churches and homes.

Unlike the more polished religious articles of European origin, *santos* immediately come across as folk art—rustic, and often naive, they show, more than a lack of formal artistic training, the unmitigated expression of their

makers' heartfelt devotion to God.

Santos and *santeros* seemed to disap-pear in the latter part of the last cen-tury, replaced by mass-produced articles that came with the railroads and the opening of New Mexico to trade from the eastern U.S. But they returned in the 1920s and 1930s as an entrepre-neurial response to the growth of inter-est in the local artistic heritage shown by outsiders. And a new generation of *santeros* has flourished again since the late sixties and early seventies, with the burgeoning interest in everything Southwestern. Among those carvers of note working today are Luis Tapia of Santa Fe, who makes very elegant inter-pretations of traditional-style painted saints; José Benjamin Lopez of Española, whose life-size, somewhat abstract images follow the form of the wood, which he usually leaves unpainted; and Eulogio and Zoraida Ortega, a husband-and-wife team from Velarde, who devotedly make smoothly carved, meticulously painted *santos* inspired by their faith and by meticu-lous historical research.

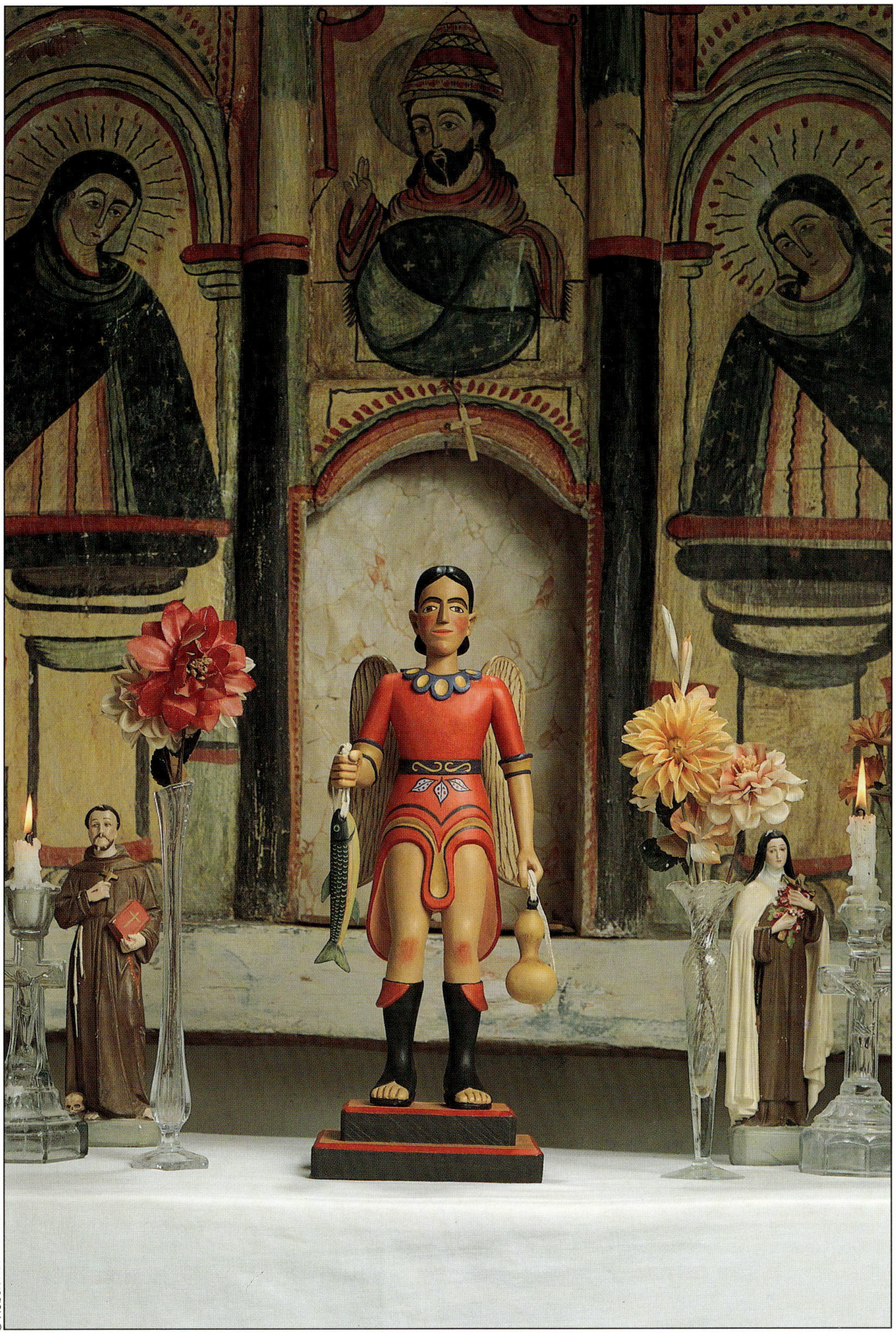

© Robert Reck

Simply and honestly carved, the saintly religious figures known as santos display the interpretive handwork of their makers. Just a few inches high, a tiny, angelic carving by Thomas L. Sena (opposite) glories in the color and texture of natural wood, while larger figures carved by Horacio Valdez (left) are painted in traditional Hispanic style.

At once ferocious-looking and endearingly naive, a lion created by David Alvarez represents some of the best work in a relatively recent New Mexican folk art form—carved and painted wooden beasts. A natural outgrowth of traditional santos, such whimsical figures have found great favor among collectors today.

Beasts

Out of the *santos* tradition has also grown a new form of New Mexican folk art—coyotes, snakes, pigs, cockerels, burros, and other native and non-native animals. These works have been popularized in recent years by exhibitions mounted by the likes of the Museum of International Folk Art and the Art Museum of South Texas at Corpus Christi, as well as by enthusiastic and perceptive dealers—most notably Santa Fe's Davis Mather.

Felipe Archuleta, a cantankerous old character out of Santa Cruz, New Mexico, is generally credited with beginning the craze around the early 1970s, and his works give off a sense of raw vitality that seems to distill the very essence of each beast. Leroy, his son, makes somewhat tamer-looking, sweeter-tempered animals. David Alvarez, one of Felipe's former apprentices, is best known for his so-called attack pigs—porkers that humorously menace with bared teeth and extended ears, tongues, and tails. Mike Rodriguez of Santa Fe carves ani-

mals that have the same rough-edged appeal as Archuleta's, though they also tend to be a touch more humorous. Santa Fe's Leroy Ortega creates animals that seem charmingly simple; many of his works, including coyotes, decorate Mark Miller's renowned Coyote Cafe. And Paul Lutonsky proves that you don't necessarily have to be Hispanic to practice the art; he specializes in wonderfully sinuous, colorfully painted snakes, many with their fangs bared.

It's surprising how reasonably priced the works of many well-known *santeros* and wood carvers can be. (It's worth noting as well that similar artworks from other countries with a Spanish colonial heritage, such as Mexico and the Philippines, may be still lower priced, while displaying some of the same decorative appeal—if not the same level of artistic accomplishment. You can find examples of these carvings in most major cities.)

So, examples from this wild menagerie of animals that rank among America's greatest examples of folk art are still within most collectors' reach.

HOW TO MAKE YOUR OWN FOLK ART SNAKE

Many Southwestern wood carvers speak of how they'll glimpse a piece of wood in nature and see in it the carving it will become. Not surprisingly, then, among the easiest of folk art animals to create is the snake, whose sinuous form inherently resides in virtually every branch and twig. Select a fallen, dry branch or twig whose shape appeals to you and is reminiscent of a snake.

Materials Needed

1 cottonwood branch or twig (pine or any other soft, workable wood can be substituted)

Carving knife

Sandpaper

Oil or water-based paint in one or more colors

Wood glue

Directions

1. With a sharp carving knife, very carefully trim the wood to give it a smoother appearance. Scrape or peel off the dried bark.

2. With the knife, always carving away from yourself, carefully taper the narrower end of the wood to form a tail. Carve the wider end into a rounded triangular shape to form the head.

3. With the tip of a smaller knife, carve a thin, shallow groove along the edge of the head to define the snake's closed mouth. If you like, carve 2 small indentations near the top front of the head for the snake's nostrils, and 2 shallow circles for the eyes on the top of the head near the sides at its widest part.

4. If you like, take one of the shavings from your carvings and carefully trim it with a small blade to make a thin, forked tongue. Carefully gouge out a small hole at the front of the mouth groove, into which the tongue will fit.

5. Use sandpaper to smooth the surface of the wood to your satisfaction. Remember: Some Southwestern artists produce fairly rough-textured work, while others opt for more refined sculptures.

6. Choose whatever palette of brightly colored paints appeals to you for the snake's body. You might paint the snake entirely 1 color, letting it dry, and then add one or more colors in a contrasting pattern of dots, spots, diamonds, blotches, or other shapes dictated by your whimsy. Or paint the snake in 2, 3, or more alternating bands of color. Then paint the eyes, nostrils, and mouth in black, outlining them in white if further contrast is needed.

7. If you've fashioned a tongue, paint it bright red. When it's dry, use wood glue to attach it securely to the mouth—forked end out, of course.

MAKING AGAVE TWINE

The tough fibers concealed in the leaves
of agave, or century plant, have long
been used by native peoples to make a
utilitarian twine, which they also weave
into workaday baskets. You could use it
to make a ristra.

Directions

*1. Dry agave leaves in the sun. (Don't try to
make twine from undried leaves; their sap
irritates the skin.)*

*2. With a rock, gently pound the leaves to
remove the outer coating from the fibers
inside.*

*3. Tie a knot in the end of the strands from
one leaf and nail it to a wall.*

*4. Divide the fibers into 2 equal strands,
holding the end of 1 in each hand.*

*5. Plait the strands, giving the righthand
strand 1 clockwise twist with each crossover.*

*6. When you come to the end of the strands,
tie another knot to secure the twine.*

Bold-yet-simple designs that show off the natural materials from which they are made pervade a wide range of traditional Southwestern crafts. Figures of people and animals, for example, decorate an Apache coil basket (near right) dating from the 1910s or 1920s. Jewelry of turquoise and silver (second right) is one of the most popular purchases for visitors to the region. Navajo sandpaintings (opposite) are traditionally a part of sacred ceremonies; but works produced for sale incorporate careful alterations to the sacred—and therefore secret—patterns.

A SAMPLER OF OTHER REGIONAL CRAFTS

While weavings, kachinas, pottery, wood carvings, and the like seem to get the bulk of the attention from connoisseurs of Southwestern crafts, a number of other creative pursuits are also well worthy of attention, including:

Basketry

Baskets are the most practical of all native Southwestern craftworks. Used for storing foods, sifting flour, cooking, gathering, carrying, and for religious ceremonies, baskets are well integrated into the daily lives of the native Southwesterners. Virtually all Southwestern peoples have practiced the art of basket making. But time and commerce have winnowed the practitioners down to just a few tribes—preeminent among them the Hopi and southern Arizona's Tohono O'odham (''Desert People''), since 1986 the official name of the tribe known in recent times as the Papago.

Fetishes

What kachinas are to the Hopi, fetishes are to the Zuni: physical embodiments of spirits, which bestow their blessings on those who possess them. But unlike kachinas, which portray men who in turn portray various spirits, fetishes are direct representations of the animals whose spirits inhabit them: stone carvings of bears, wolves, sheep, eagles, mountain lions, and so on. Hunting fetishes, used to ensure a successful hunt, often have small arrowheads bound to the animals' backs.

Jewelry

The Zuni, the Hopi, and the Navajo all practice the art of jewelry making in silver embellished with turquoise and other semiprecious stones. Mosaiclike Zuni jewelry features the art of inlaying stones into a silver base or setting cut stones or nuggets in silver; Zuni fetishes also appear in their jewelry, often in miniature and strung as beads on necklaces. Hopi jewelry is noted for the art of overlay, in which cutout designs of silver are soldered atop silver bases. Navajo jewelry is predominantly cast from molten silver or hammered and stamped with intricate designs.

Sand Paintings

True sand paintings last no more than about twelve hours. Created as part of Navajo religious ceremonies, these intricate patterns of colored sand are begun at sunrise, completed during the day's observances, and eliminated before the day is over. But in recent decades, tribal artists have begun to create sand paintings in which certain colors or details are changed to avoid transgressing on sacred designs.

Storytellers

A fairly recent offshoot of Pueblo pottery, these popular figures—portraying a seated adult, mouth open in mid-tale, swarmed by small, enraptured children—got their start with Cochiti potter Helen Cordero, who was commissioned by Alexander Girard to elaborate on one of her mother-and-child pieces. Now many potters in New Mexico and Arizona produce such works.

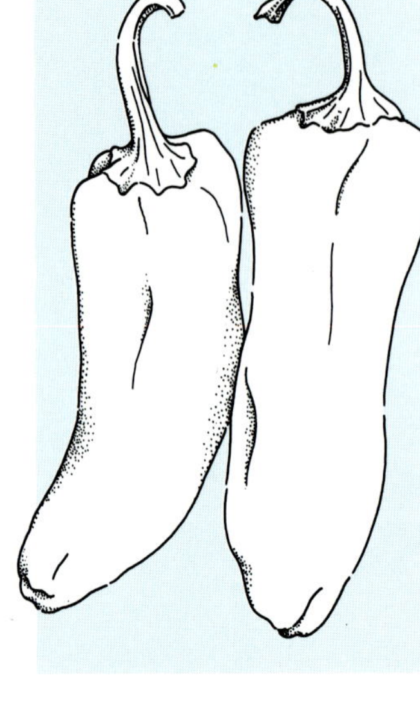

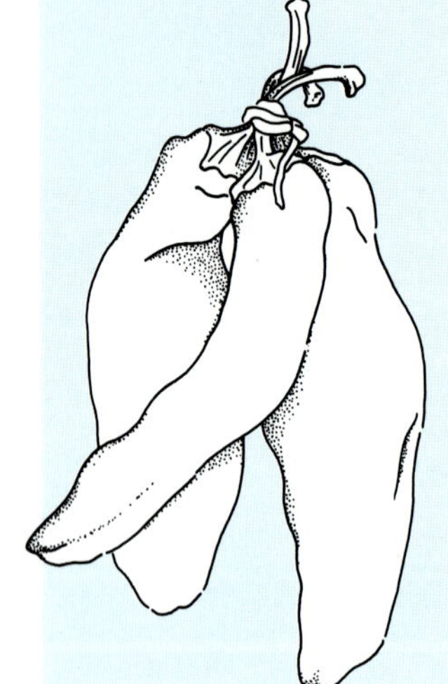

1

MAKING A RISTRA

While making the long strings of dried red chiles known as ristras is basically a culinary task, no different in its way from putting up preserves, the resulting objects have such decorative appeal that they amount to a folk craft in their own right.

It's easy to make your own ristras at home. Choose whole, fresh, perfectly unblemished red Anaheim chile pods, and vary the amount depending on the size of the ristra you want to make. But one word of caution: If your home climate is more humid than the desert of the Southwest, your ristras are more likely to grow mold than to dry. If that's the case, you might simply like to make a ristra from predried whole red chile pods.

Materials Needed

2 to 3 dozen fresh whole chile pods (dried pods are another option)

8 feet of twine or straw

Directions

1. Take 3 chile pods and a piece of straw or heavy cotton twine about 6 inches long. Wind the straw or twine around the stems of the three pods to bind them together, tying it in a secure knot. Repeat with the remaining chiles, 3 at a time.

2. Take a piece of straw or twine several feet long and, starting about 8 inches from one end, securely tie one bunch of chiles to it. A few inches further along the string, tie the next, so that the first bunch overlaps the second by about half the length of the chiles. Continue until all the chiles are tied to the string.

3. Hang the ristra in a dry, airy place; in the Southwest, they are traditionally hung under the eaves of the house. Leave it there until the pods are thoroughly dry, up to several weeks; inspect it regularly, and carefully remove any pods that show signs of mold.

4. Hang the ristra wherever you like for a decorative effect. The chiles will stay beautiful for several years, though they are best used for cooking—pulled or cut from the ristra— within about a year.

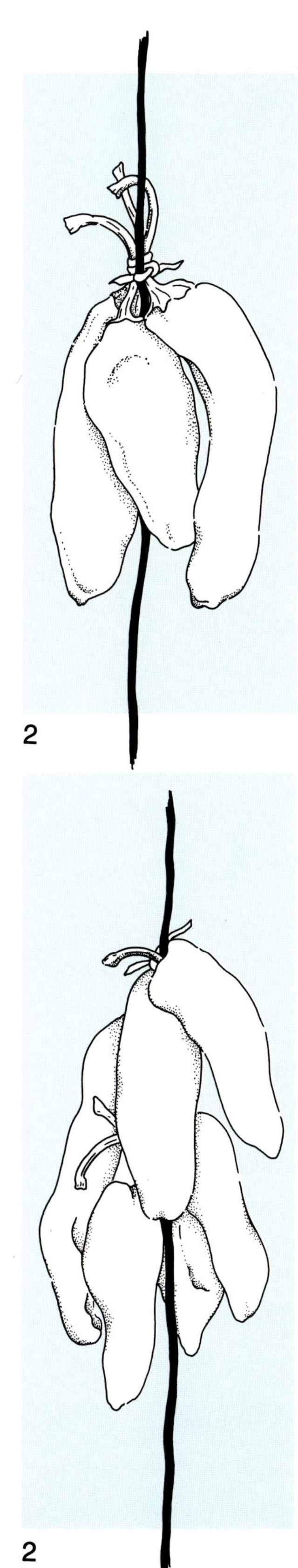

103

Antique Native American crafts of the Southwest are exquisite objects richly steeped in tradition and history. A picture bowl created in the black-on-white Mimbres style (right), which first flourished from about the tenth through the twelfth centuries A.D., includes a "kill hole." Kill holes were usually struck through the bottoms of pottery pieces that were buried in graves. Dating from the 1880s to about 1910, a group of pueblo historic pots (opposite, top) displays a variety of distinctive styles, while the headdress worn by a kachina dancer (opposite, bottom) combines the beauty of craftsmanship with deep ceremonial meaning.

COLLECTING NATIVE SOUTHWESTERN ANTIQUES

Enter any home in Southern California where Southwestern artifacts are seriously collected, and more likely than not at least some of the pieces will have come from Philip Garaway's Native American Art Gallery in the Los Angeles beach community of Venice.

As a teenager in the early 1970s, Garaway lived on the Navajo Reservation in the Monument Valley–Four Corners area with his parents, who both taught there. Out of that experience grew his love for native Southwestern arts, and he soon began to collect and sell them. Since it opened in 1983, his gallery has maintained a high reputation for dealing exclusively in museum-quality pieces, and he maintains strong ties to collectors and other dealers nationwide and around the world.

Garaway has seen Native American art of the Southwest grow from an esoteric pursuit among collectors to one that has witnessed tremendous growth and ever-increasing prices. Take, for

example, a November 1989 sale at Sotheby's in New York of pieces from the collection of the late Edwin Janss, Jr., one of the most noted private collectors of Southwestern native arts. A classic Mimbres black-on-white picture bowl, dating from around A.D. 950–1150, was expected to sell for around $25,000 to $35,000; it actually went for $82,500. And a rare Navajo man's wearing blanket from around 1830–1840 had an estimated selling price of $100,000 to $150,000, but finally sold for $522,500.

Garaway is eager to stress that potential collectors shouldn't be put off by these high prices. "The pieces that get the most publicity are the ones that sell for the most," he says. "And as with any collectibles, the top end always appreciates more than the lower end. Truly great objects are going to cost a lot of money." That doesn't mean, though, that you can't get started collecting some quality pieces for an outlay in the low three figures—or less.

Ten Important Tips

Whatever the price range you're collecting in, Garaway offers these pointers to help you get started:

Educate yourself. "The first thing I like to sell people is a book," says Garaway. Do your homework on Southwestern art. Go to museums. Buy scholarly works and auction catalogs. Read about the kinds of pieces that interest you. "Expose your eye to as many items as possible." With time, your eye will become more sophisticated and discerning.

Buy what you love. "Good art grows on you," says Garaway. "If you buy what you love, five years from now you'll love it even more."

Buy the best within your price range. Determine in advance how much you want to spend on a particular kind of piece. Then seek out the very best pieces of their kind for the money— rather than, say, buying a poor example of some kind of artifact that is generally much higher priced. "And it's better to buy one really good piece," Garaway emphasizes, "than half a dozen little, less important pieces." Also, he adds, it's important to stay level-headed when starting out, though you shouldn't be afraid to get your feet wet. "Make your mistakes early, while you're still learning and still collecting at the bottom end of your budget. They could be cheap lessons in the long run."

Be aware of the nature of your investment. Though Native American art can be a good investment, you must be aware that it's a long-term, not-very-liquid one. "If you're prepared to live with it and love it," says Garaway, "in the long range it will most likely grow in value."

Shop around. As part of your continuing education process, compare the pieces and the prices offered by different dealers. Ask them questions. And buy from people who make you feel comfortable, who seem completely up front and straight with you.

Buy from a reputable dealer. Whatever dealer you purchase art from should guarantee a piece's authenticity, tell you about any restoration work that has been done to it, and if possible provide its provenance—the piece's particular history. Garaway, for example, provides a certificate of authenticity, along with any other information he is able to gather, on every piece he sells.

Set some parameters for your collecting. "People today are eclectic," says Garaway, "and this art goes with all environments. So be aware that you can own just a few pieces and still be satisfied without having to acquire an entire collection." But should you feel a calling to collect seriously, he advises, you should formulate a plan for the kind of collection you want to build. Do you want to collect only baskets, say, or Navajo rugs? Within that genre, do you want one piece from each different period, or do you want comprehensive examples of different styles and motifs? Not only does this make collecting more interesting and exciting for you, he says, but it also builds in a greater sense of accomplishment. "Someday in the future, you'll have done something—you'll have made a personal statement of your particular interest."

Beware of fakes. Be cautious of really great-looking deals in out-of-the-way places, such as roadside stands. While you may make great discoveries in odd places, you might also get taken. Again, says Garaway, you should do your homework in advance—even down to learning the subtle changes that have taken place over the years in a particular genre of artwork: a difference of twenty years in the dating of a piece may mean a difference of many thousands of dollars in its price. In the long run it may be wiser for you to pay a little bit more to a reputable dealer.

Consider collecting antiques. Many collectors get great pleasure and satisfaction from contemporary Native American pieces—particularly those produced by name artists who either emulate tribal traditions dating back hundreds or thousands of years or who innovate in bold new directions. Other collectors, including Garaway, prefer antique Native American art. "It's one of a kind," says Garaway, "and many pieces aren't any more expensive than contemporary works." He points out as well that antiques are generally much easier to resell because of their rarity, and they usually appreciate faster. What's more, says Garaway, "there's a certain magical quality" to an antique piece, which provides its collector with a "primal link to America's native heritage."

Don't be afraid to live with the art. Some Native American artworks are still not only perfectly functional but also sturdy enough to stand up to practical use. Navajo rugs, for example, may well most often be hung on the wall like art these days; but, says Garaway, "they still hold up on the floor—and look great there."

SOUTHWESTERN GARDENS

Some people scoff at the idea of calling the yards surrounding Southwestern homes "gardens." That reaction is borne out by Edward Abbey's description of southeastern Utah in his enthralling book Desert Solitaire. *"I have called it a garden," he wrote, "and it is— a rock garden. Despite the great variety of living things to be found here, most of the surface of the land, at least three-quarters of it, is sand or sandstone, naked, monolithic, austere, and unadorned as the sculpture of the moon."*

And that's precisely the kind of beauty one learns to appreciate and love in the gardens of the Southwest. A front or back yard may be mostly sand, rocks, and cacti, but in that very austerity, it's a microcosm of the great desert wilderness just beyond the garden wall. And like that wilderness, it may also encompass plants of rare and wistful beauty—the gnarled mesquite, the agave, or century plant, that blooms once in its lifetime and then dies, the wildflowers that blossom in a dazzling burst and then disappear as rapidly as they arrived.

Odd as it may seem at first, the appreciation of Southwestern gardens may be likened to that of Japanese rock gardens. Minimalism is at work here: a sense of striving to paint a private landscape every bit as beautiful as nature's own broad canvas, of creating perfection with the barest of essentials. And once you've shifted your focus and attuned yourself to the desert's stark beauty—whether within the confines of your own patch of land or out among the vast stretches of the Southwest—you may well find yourself approaching a sense of serenity, of peace, that is Zenlike in its quiet intensity.

110

There's an austere
beauty to the
Southwestern garden
that, not surprisingly,
is perfectly compan-
ionable with the
region's stark geol-
ogy and its earthen
architecture. In a
Santa Fe courtyard,
for example, a spiky-
leafed agave (page
108) lends sharp
punctuation to the
rocks and rounded
archway. The red
flowers of the appro-
priately named
cherry sage (Salvia
greggii), shown here,
stand out dramati-
cally against a worn
adobe wall.

111

112

THE NATURAL BEAUTY OF THE DESERT SOUTHWEST

So vast is the Southwest (to be precise, 423,434 square miles in Arizona, Colorado, New Mexico, and Utah alone) that the mind may well boggle at the thought of trying to take in, let alone comprehend, all of its natural beauty. But one spot in particular admirably achieves that daunting goal in just 110 acres of Sonora Desert foothills, fourteen miles west of Tucson, Arizona.

First opened in 1952, the Arizona-Sonora Desert Museum has been acclaimed as one of the ten best zoos in the world. And it is that, with magnificent outdoor habitats for desert creatures from coyotes to mountain lions, bears to bighorn sheep. A marvelous aviary allows visitors to walk among some eighty species of colorful bird life, and a separate hummingbird habitat lets you get nose to beak with eight different iridescent hummingbird species. Creepier desert denizens—scorpions, rattlesnakes, and the like—reside safely behind glass in insect and reptile displays. There are also geology exhibits

that explain how the region was formed and displays of the gems and precious metals that lie beneath its surface.

But most fascinating of all, perhaps, is the way in which the museum embraces the full range of natural desert vegetation: mountain environments of cottonwood, cypress, ash, pine, and fir; grasslands covered in wild grains and dotted with creosote, ocotillo, and palo verde; *bajadas,* the debris-strewn lower slopes of desert mountains, where cactus, palo verde, mesquite, and ironwood grow among wildflower-strewn slopes; and the searing flatlands, where only the most drought-resistant plants—primarily creosote and cactus—punctuate the soil and sand. In addi-

tion, a series of trails at the heart of the museum meanders through cactus and succulent gardens, filled with superb specimens that are especially beautiful in late spring, when many are in bloom; and a separate exhibit examines the role of the saguaro cactus in desert life.

In conjunction with *Sunset Magazine,* the museum has also developed an area called the Demonstration Desert Garden, which provides a wealth of inspiration to the home landscaper. Filled with native plants, it is to the Arizona-Sonora Desert Museum as a whole what the museum itself is to the great Southwest: a neat, comprehensive, and beautiful microcosm of desert life. It's well worth a visit.

Wildflowers in the Desert

To many people, wildflowers seem the greatest miracle of desert life. They usually bloom after the first spring rains, blanketing the landscape of sand and rocks in a seemingly endless succession and variety of different shapes and col-ors until autumn. Wildflower lovers can admire the plants in their natural state or, if they are Southwest residents, grow them in a home garden. If the latter is the case, do not collect specimens from the wild, as many of these plants are protected by law.

Some wildflowers cannot wait for spring and begin to decorate the land-

Texas state flower and only grows a foot or so high; it is a particularly stunning lupine, often with a white or yellow spot on its petals.

From the end of winter until mid-spring, wildflower aficionados also delight in nama (*Nama* spp.). This delicate plant has tiny purple bell-shaped flowers very close to the ground.

Around Easter time, you might observe the ajo-lily (*Hesperocallis undulata*), named for its white lilylike blossoms which bloom 2 to 3 inches wide on stalks as high as 6 feet. Not quite as showy as the ajo-lily, bladderpod (*Lesquerella gordoni*) has diminutive bright yellow flowers that grow several to a stem up to 1 foot high. The plant's name derives from the appearance of the seed pods, which look like miniature inflated bladders. Look for bladderpod from late winter to early spring.

Another spring flower, evening primrose (*Oenothera* spp.), displays showy white, yellow, or pink blossoms at night or on overcast days. Identify the plant by its four double-tipped petals, which form a cup shape nearly 2 inches wide on stems reaching 3 feet. Sacred datura (*Datura* spp.) is also a nighttime bloomer, and its white trumpet-shaped flowers span 6 inches across. The plant also blossoms after rainfall. The foliage emits a poison, so be careful around this plant, which is common from late spring until fall.

Royal blue, delicate-looking larkspur (*Delphinium* spp.) blossoms appear throughout the springtime. The flowers grow in spiral form on the 2-foot-high stalks. The foliage of the larkspurs emits a poisonous juice, so again be careful when handling this plant.

Globe mallow (*Sphaeralcea* spp.) is a five-petaled flower with a poppylike shape. The flowers can be colored peach, red, white, or purple and grow on a hairy stem that is irritating to the touch and can reach heights of 5 feet. Look for it in springtime.

Owl's clover (*Orthocarpus purpurascens*) and phlox (*Phlox* spp.) delight

scape in winter. Lupine (*Lupinus* spp.) flowers, which range in color from pale blue to purple, appear as early as January and continue to bloom until May. They grow up to 2 feet high; multiple showy blossoms densely cover each stalk. Beware the seeds, however, as they are quite poisonous. One species, the bluebonnet (*L. subcarnosus*), is the

The five-petaled wildflowers known as phlox, whose colors range from white and pink to lilac and deeper purple, adds its own bright cheer to the desert scene throughout the springtime.

115

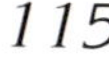

LIGHTING THE CHRISTMAS PATHWAY

Every Christmas throughout the Southwest, front gardens and public pathways light up with a charming custom dating back to Spain, when small lanterns (farolitos) or bonfires (luminarias) would be lit to guide pilgrims seeking the Christ child. Today, both Spanish terms refer to little lanterns made from school lunch-size brown paper bags, which make their appearance just before the holidays and especially on Christmas Eve.

With their tops folded down about an inch to help hold their sides straight, the bags are filled with one to two inches of sand. Into the center of the sand, a small votive candle is pressed, and the bags are placed a few feet apart along home garden walks, in public gardens and plazas, outside churches, and along the tops of adobe walls. Once lit, the candles give off a rich, warm, diffused glow through the brown paper, a look that complements the stark beauty of Southwestern gardens and the rustic charm of the architecture.

Southwesterners from early to late spring. The former has purple flowers with yellow spots growing on 16-inch spikes. Phlox's color palette—white, pink, lilac, or purple—adds a touch of delicacy to the desert; the plant grows up to 3 feet high, and each flower is five-petaled.

From mid-spring until fall, delicate, vivid yellow senna flowers (*Senna covesii*) brighten the desert; the stalks can grow to 2 feet. Pale yellow desert zinnias (*Zinnia grandiflora*) also blossom during this period. They have bright orange centers and grow on 8-inch stalks.

Fanciful-looking mariposa (*Calochortus* spp.) blossoms in April. Its three-petaled flowers—which can be white, golden yellow, or orange—are quite attractive and take their name from the Spanish word for "butterfly." The plant grows to 8 inches high and has four flowers on a single stalk. April is also the month when the prickly poppy (*Argemone arizonica*) makes its first appearance; it continues to bloom until July. The floppy, 3-inch-wide white petals of this flower enclose a large cluster of yellow stamens—inspiring the vivid nickname "cowboy's fried egg." The 3- to 4-foot-tall stems are quite prickly to the touch, and the yellow juice emitted by the plant is quite poisonous—so it's best to admire this plant from afar.

Come summer, the Southwest desert renews itself with a new burst of blooms. In late June, purple prairie clover (*Petalostemon purpureum*) appears. Individual, tiny pink or purple flowers with conical heads perch atop 2-foot-tall stems. Blue flax (*Linum* spp.) soon follows, with abundant, five-petaled blue flowers growing on stems up to 2 feet high; the blooming period extends to early fall.

In July and August, columbine (*Aquilegia* spp.) adds a grace note to the landscape. These pretty little yellow and blue flowers, up to 3 inches in width, have elegant trailing sepals that resemble birds in flight (their name comes from the Latin word for "dove"). The month of August also is brightened by the bush morning glory (*Ipomoea leptophylla*), whose magenta trumpet-shaped flowers bloom only in the early morning and the evening. These plants grow to 3 feet high.

From July through October, the simple yellow flowers of the desert poppy (*Eschscholtzia* spp.) emerge. The blossoms are yellow with a deep red or orange center and grow 1 to 2 feet high.

As if some giant child had spilled its paintbox across the desert floor, Southwestern wildflowers bring color to the region throughout the year, from the pristine white of evening primrose (opposite) to the blue of the mountain delphinium (left).

117

*The roses of the desert
are the cactus flowers,
crystal of translucent
yellow or of rose-
colour. But set
among spines the
devil himself must
have conceived in a
moment of sheer
ecstasy.*
—D.H. Lawrence,
St. Mawr

Cactus Flowers

Some would argue that cactus flowers are the Southwest's most astonishing floral display. The flowers appear in spring and summer.

The flat pads of beavertail cactus erupt in vivid pink blossoms, as if someone had sneaked up and strewn them with tissue paper. A stout barrel cactus suddenly wears a crown of bright orange flowers. The tops of tall saguaros disappear beneath a profusion—some three hundred in a six-week season—of waxy, trumpet-shaped blooms (Arizona's state flower) that together are remarkably reminiscent of a gaudy, fifties-style bathing cap.

As with any flower, those of cacti attract airborne creatures—usually bees, but also bats and sometimes birds—that pollinate them, giving rise to fruit that contain the seeds responsible for the species' survival. For that reason, cactus flowers on public lands, like all wildflowers, are closely protected by state and federal laws. The best way to enjoy them is to observe, sketch, and photograph—but not remove—them.

The beauty of the Southwest's wild plants invites close-up appreciation through the camera's lens. Desert or Indian paintbrush (right), for example, looks as if its bracts and calyx had been dipped in bright pigment (the actual flowers of this plant are concealed within). The plant known by the scientific name Calliandra pennsularis *(right, below) displays a cluster of multiple stamens that inspire its more common appellation: fairy-duster.*

Photographing Wildflowers

So fragile is the Southwest's desert environment that it's wisest to refrain there from the popular hobby of picking wildflowers. But there's another excellent way to bring home the specimens you spot when rambling through the region, a method that ensures that the flowers' beauty will stay fresh and vibrant forever: photography.

Your needs for photographing wildflowers are fairly simple:

- *A camera for close-up work*. This could be a 35-mm camera with a macro lens, or one of the new range of electric zoom cameras that allow you to shoot close-ups. Alternatively, you may just be content with shooting still lifes or landscape shots—whole bushes or cacti in bloom, or a field of wildflowers.

- *Slow film*. Whether you're shooting slides or prints, use film with an ASA of 100 or lower, so their fine grain will give you sharp images.

- *A tripod*. Though not essential, this is a good idea for steadying the camera to get good, crisp close-ups of flowers—particularly if you're using slow film.

- *A piece of black velvet*. Placed on the ground beyond the flower you're shooting, or draped on a stand placed behind it, this can provide a dramatic backdrop that—especially if the natural background is very busy—will highlight the flower's beauty.

- *Kneepads and a blanket*. You may well find yourself getting down on the ground to get the best shot.

- *A notebook*. Like most students of nature and photography buffs, you'll want to jot down the what, when, where, and how for future reference.

120

STATE	NICKNAME	ORIGIN
Arizona	Grand Canyon State	Spanish version of Pima Indian word for "little spring place" or Aztec word *arizuma*, meaning "silver-bearing."
Nevada	Sagebrush State	Spanish, meaning "snow-clad."
New Mexico	Land of Enchantment	Spaniards in Mexico applied term to land north and west of Rio Grande in the 16th century.
Utah	Beehive State	A Navajo word meaning upper, or higher up, as applied to a Shoshone tribe called Ute. Spanish form is Yutta, English form is Uta or Utah.
Colorado	Centennial State, Silver State	From the Spanish for "red," after the red banks of the Colorado river.

122

FLOWER	*BIRD*	*TREE*
Blossom of the Saguaro Cactus	Cactus Wren	Palo Verde
Sagebrush	Mountain Bluebird	Single-leaf Piñon
Yucca	Roadrunner	Piñon
Sego lily	Seagull	Blue Spruce
Rocky Mountain Columbine	Lark Bunting	Colorado Blue Spruce

Familiar local sights in nature have come to be closely—and officially—associated with particular Southwestern states, among them Utah's sego lily (opposite) and the mountain bluebird of Nevada (left).

*O*ver the centuries, natives of the Southwest have found myriad practical uses for the local plantlife. The agave (right), for example, has an edible heart beneath its spiny exterior, and yields products as diverse as tequila and a kind of hand-woven twine. Cottonwood trees (opposite) provide, among other things, the primary raw material for the region's woodcarvers.

124

Ten Typical Southwestern Garden Plants

It's easy to fall into the trap of thinking that every plant growing in the Southwest is a cactus. Here are a few of the other easily cultivated plants that, through both their beauty and their usefulness, contribute to the region's unique character:

Agave
(Agave americana)

Also known as the century plant, this spiky-leafed, rosette-shaped member of the amaryllis family takes many years—from seven to around forty—to produce its single flower, on a stalk that can reach an incredible 35 feet in height. Once it flowers, the plant dies. Native Americans roast and eat the agave's heart and its flower stem. The plant's juices are fermented to make tequila. And fibers in the plant's leaves may be unraveled and used to make twine (*see page 99*) from which baskets may be woven.

Chamiso
(Atriplex spp.)

The saltbush to those of us not from the Southwest, this low, dense, blue-green shrub grows wild throughout the region, and also makes an excellent ornamental garden plant. Native Americans also used to eat the plant's seeds.

Cottonwood
(Populus spp.)

These crown-shaped shade trees with spade-shaped, bright green leaves grow along streambeds throughout the Southwest. Their relatively soft wood is the medium of choice for many *santeros* and folk-art carvers of the region. Cottonwood is also used for building, and Native Americans weave its small branches into baskets.

Creosote
(Larrea tridentata)

This beautiful desert shrub has ornamental-looking, sculptural branches, dark evergreen leaves, and small yellow flowers. After the rain, you can smell their camphorous resin—traditionally used as a Native American antiseptic or antibiotic.

Ironwood
(Olneya tesota)

As its name implies, the ironwood tree produces one of the world's finest, heaviest hardwoods, used by Southwest natives not only for building and carving, but also for making farming tools and even arrowheads. The tree itself grows up to 30 feet in height, and in springtime it sports small, white to pink flowers against its gray-green leaves.

Mesquite
(Prosopis spp.)

In the Southwest, this beautifully gnarled, shrublike tree is regarded as nothing less than "the tree of life." We've all grown familiar in recent years with mesquite charcoal or wood, whose intense heat and subtle aroma has transformed the art of grilling in America. Cooking aside, mesquite also makes excellent firewood, and it is also widely used for construction. The soft inner bark is woven into baskets or distilled—along with the sap, pitch, and leaves—to make native medicines. The pitch is also used to decorate pottery, the gum is turned into candy, the fibers of its long roots are wound into cord, and the bean pods—ground into a flour— have long been a staple of the native diet. The mesquite's blossoms, incidentally, provide bees with the raw materials for producing outstanding honey that is both aromatic and flavorful.

Ocotillo
(Fouquieria splendens)

Often mistaken for a cactus, this woody succulent is used as a wonderful living garden fence—strong enough to keep animals out—by people who plant a row of cuttings close to each other and wire their tops together.

Palo Verde
(Cercidium spp.)

Perhaps the Southwest's prettiest tree, the palo verde has an almost wistful quality to it. The slender, somewhat gnarled greenish or blue-green trunks, branches, and delicate leaves seem to sweep upward toward the sky. In the spring, they're often covered as well with delicate yellow blossoms. The tree's seeds have been a popular food for native peoples: when green, their flavor resembles peas; dried and ground, they are reminiscent of peanuts.

Piñon
(Pinus cembroides)

The piñon's cones are the source of the Southwest's most popular nut. This twisted, tough-looking pine seems to embody the rugged beauty of the region.

Yucca
(Yucca spp.)

These striking members of the lily family (and relatives of the agave) grow to a treelike stature, their branches topped by clusters of long, narrow, spiky leaves. Their graceful white blossoms, reminiscent of some orchids in their color and shape, have a delicate flavor and crisp texture that make them excellent as salad additions; the young flower stalks as well are often cooked and eaten. The banana yucca produces a sweet fruit, shaped vaguely like a banana. The soap-tree yucca's stems and roots also yield up a sudsy lather, which Native Americans of the region once used as their soap. Like the agave, the yucca's fibrous leaves provide the raw materials for cords and baskets.

Each spring the ocotillo (opposite) bursts out in particularly sweet, edible flowers, which are a favorite of hummingbirds. From the cones of the scruffy-looking piñon (above) comes the most popular nut of the Southwest. Certain species of yucca (left) produce tasty blossoms, flower stalks, and fruit.

I*t's not hard to imagine why denizens of the Southwest ascribe a near-human nobility to the saguaro: The cactus' long, curving branches often take on the sensuous look of a living person.*

128

THE SAGUARO

In her 1924 masterpiece on the Southwest, *The Land of Journeys' Ending,* Mary Austin captured in just a few paragraphs the essence of the saguaro's mystique. (It's important to note right away that at the time she wrote, the phonetically accurate spelling of ''sahuaro'' was in common use among Anglos.)

Stately. Ancient. Immense. Resilient. Secretive. Solitary. All these qualities belong to the mightiest of cacti. And so powerfully does the saguaro embody them that it has become the symbol for virtually all of Southwestern desert plant life—despite the fact that the saguaro lives only in Arizona and the adjacent Mexican state of Sonora, with a few strays found across the California border.

To see them at their finest, though, you've got to drive outside of Tucson toward Saguaro National Monument, just beyond the Arizona-Sonora Desert Museum. In this 83,000-acre preserve, established in 1933, thousands of saguaros cover the desert floor and the mountainsides. ''Nowhere in the world is there so fine a stand,'' commented Dr. Homer L. Shantz, who was instrumental in founding the saguaro reserve. ''Here the plants rise so close together that at times it is difficult to see through them for any great distance.'' From certain vantage points, especially at sunrise or sunset, the saguaros resemble a surreal urban skyline, reinforcing Frank Lloyd Wright's famous observation, ''The saguaro is the greatest example of a skyscraper that was ever built.''

Going west by the Old Trails Road, you do not begin to find sahuaro until you are well down toward the black hills of Tucson, and it is not at its best this side of the toadlike heap of volcanic trap which turns the river out of its course, called Tummomoc. Here it rises to a height of twenty-five or thirty feet, erect, columnar, dull green, and deeply fluted, the outer ridges of the flutings set with rows of lateral spines that inclose it as in a delicate grayish web. Between the ridges the sahuaro has a texture like well-surfaced leather, giving back the light like spears, that, seen from a rapidly moving car, make a continuous vertical flicker in the landscape. Marching together against the rose-and-vermilion evening, they have a stately look, like the pillars of ruined temples.

For the first hundred years or so the sahuaro preserves the outline of its virgin intention to be straight, but in the case of wounding, or perhaps in seasons of excess, it puts forth without calculation immense columnar branches like the arms of candelabra, curving to bring their growing tips parallel to the axis of the main stem, which they reproduce as if from their own roots....

*—Mary Austin,
The Land of
Journeys' Ending*

Saguaro Stats

A few superlatives to consider:

• Only 1 out of every 275,000 saguaro seeds ever grows to maturity.

• Saguaros grow in an elevation range from 700 to 3,500 feet above sea level.

• A 30-year-old saguaro measures, on average, about 6 feet in height.

• A mature saguaro may reach a height of 50 feet and weigh up to 12 tons.

• Mature saguaros have shallow root systems that may extend up to 70 feet in diameter, and are capable of taking in up to 1 ton of water after a brief rain.

• Seventeen to 28 woody ribs support the saguaro's pleated flesh, which expands or contracts as the cactus absorbs or uses up water.

• Woodpeckers, flickers, owls, and other birds excavate holes between the ribs to make sheltered nests, which, when deserted, are taken over by mice and other desert creatures.

• Saguaros have a maximum life span of approximately 200 years.

• Saguaros don't start to branch out until they're around 75 years old, and a very old saguaro may have as many as 50 branching arms.

• Twenty to 25 spines ranging from $^{1}/_{2}$ to 3 inches in length grow from each cluster or areole.

• A large saguaro will produce up to 100 flowers in a brief 1-month season in May or June.

• The saguaro's edible, sweet, juicy, 2-inch-long fruits hold up to 2,000 seeds each.

• Saguaros stolen from public lands sell at prices in excess of $1,000 to people who use them for landscaping. Often, a cactus will die when put in a strange environment. The wild saguaro population is severely threatened.

The word "cactus" seems so specific that it often obscures the amazing diversity that actually exists among this family of plants, from tiny cacti no bigger than your thumb to the various members of the slender, ribless cholla family (above) to the mighty saguaro (right).

The voice that beautifies the land!
The voice above,
The voice of the thunder
Within the dark cloud
Again and again it sounds,
The voice that beautifies the land.
The voice that beautifies the land!
The voice below;
The voice of the grasshopper
Among the plants
Again and again it sounds,
The voice that beautifies the land.
    —"Twelfth Song of the Thunder," *Navajo Mountain Chant, translated by Washington Matthews, 1883*

131

A Cactus Gallery

While saguaros are far and away the most prominent cacti of the Southwest, by no means are they the only ones. More than seventy different species of cactus share the desert, most of which are also adaptable to the home landscape. Herewith, some brief profiles of the most prominent and pleasing specimens. Some of the names, as you will see, denote groups of cacti within which there are many different varieties; others refer to single species; all, delightfully, have aptly descriptive names.

Barrel
(Ferocactus spp.)

Round, stout, and vaguely shaped and sized like a barrel, these are the cacti that hold water better than most other species. The spiny variety is taller, more slender, and covered with very nasty-looking spines; the many-headed barrel grows in low-lying clusters; wooly-headed barrels are topped by a pad of woollike hairs that protect their growing tips from direct sunshine.

Beavertail
(Opuntia basilaris)

A cactus measuring up to 1 foot tall, composed of multiple gray- or blue-green pads shaped like the tail of a beaver.

Cholla
(Opuntia spp.)

A group of sinuous-looking, treelike cacti with no ribs, almost completely covered with spines. The buckhorn or major variety resembles deer antlers; the staghorn or tree cholla are similarly branched; the youngest joints of the jumping cholla practically jump off the plant with a gust of wind or a nearby footstep; pencil chollas have long, thin, pencillike joints; the appealing teddy bear variety looks plump and cuddly, though it will stick you as badly as any cactus.

Cream
(Mamilaria spp.)

These low-lying, flat little cacti may get their name from their cream-colored flowers or from the fact that, when cut, they emit a creamy-looking juice.

132

Hedgehog
(Echinocereus spp.)

As the name implies, these little cacti
are about the size and shape of their
namesakes. The strawberry type produces berry-sized, sweet fruits; purple
hedgehogs have a purplish green skin;
comb hedgehogs get their name from
their closely spaced rows of spines.

Night-Blooming Cereus
(Nyctocereus serpentinus)

The stems of this gray, skinny, many-
branched cactus may seem dead for
most of the year, though some aficionados find in it the same appeal I
guess as a piece of driftwood. But
come early summer, for no more than a
week, the cactus bursts into white
blooms, each of which opens in early
evening and is dead come morning.

Organ Pipe
(Pachycereus marginatus)

Resembling arrays of theater-organ
pipes, these giants grow as tall as
25 feet.

Pincushion
(Coryphantha spp.)

Like a seamstress's pincushion, this
little species—no more than 6 inches
high—is covered in pinlike spines.

Prickly Pear
(Opuntia spp.)

Undoubtedly the most common cacti
of the Southwest, the many varieties of
these rambling plants are all made up of
flat pads contoured vaguely like pears
or oblongs. The name also refers to the
cacti's sweet fruit.

Because I was one of the youngest, I may today be the only one left of that band to tell of the old, old trail that, like a rainbow, led us westward… .

Scenes of the old trail come flooding back to me: Places where the earth was like a Persian rug, the lavender, red and yellow wildflowers mingling with the silvery green prairie grass.

—Marian Sloane Russell, Land of Enchantment: Memoirs of Marian Russell Along the Santa Fe Trail

GROWING YOUR OWN CACTI

However appealing the thought of a Southwestern garden might be, not all of us live in an arid climate. And though some foolhardy Southwesterners may, through diligent hard work and misuse of precious water, make a lush garden grow in the desert, the reverse just won't work: too much rain or too much cold would destroy a home landscape of desert plants in a non-desert locale.

But, fortunately, it's fairly easy to make cacti thrive almost anywhere indoors, and nurseries nationwide sell good, small specimens of potted cactus. You'll find countless books that will tell you at great length how to take care of them, but here are some basics to get you started:

1. Mixing the soil. Contrary to popular belief, cacti don't grow in sand alone, which holds no nutrients. While individual species' needs may vary, a basic dependable potting mixture consists of equal parts coarse sand (fine beach sand holds water too well, preventing proper drainage), garden loam, and fine, well-decomposed leaf mold, tossed together with a little crushed charcoal.

2. Choosing the pot. Select a glazed terra-cotta pot with a good-size drainage hole. The pot's circumference should be slightly larger than that of the cactus, including spines. Place the pot inside a dish to catch water that drains off.

3. Potting. For drainage, put a 1-inch layer of clean pebbles or broken pot pieces in the bottom of the pot, then cover with a layer of coarse gravel, topped by some charcoal or moss. Add enough dry potting soil mixture to support the cactus's roots. Handling the cactus carefully with tongs, steady it in the pot while you add the remaining soil to support the plant's base $1/2$ to 1 inch below the rim of the pot. Top with a thin layer of coarse gravel.

4. Selecting a warm and well-lit spot. The best spot for most indoor cacti is near a window with plenty of natural light and some direct sunlight; full, day-long, direct sun is not necessary. A window ledge, window shelves, or a greenhouse window are all ideal places for growing and displaying cacti. Give each pot a quarter turn at the same time daily, so the cacti will grow evenly. In very cold climates, heating is desirable to keep the cacti at a comfortable temperature year round, though most cacti are used to winter temperatures as low as 50 degrees F.

5. Watering. During summer, water cacti thoroughly—enough to soak through the soil without leaving any water in the drainage dish. Then don't water again until the soil has become almost—but not entirely—dry; intervals will depend on the individual cactus, the weather, and the size of the pot.

6. Resting. As fall approaches, gradually cut down on the watering. Water very seldom from mid-fall to early spring. Such a rest period is a natural part of the cactus's life cycle.

7. Repotting. When the growing season begins again, consider repotting your cacti to slightly larger pots, with fresh soil mixture to nourish them for another year.

Appendix

Contact landmarks in advance for hours; write to mail-order companies for catalog and merchandise information.

Architectural Landmarks

Arcosanti
Cordes Junction
Mayer, AZ 86333

Baca & Bloom Houses Pioneer Museum
300 East Main Street
P.O. Box 472
Trinidad, CO 81082

Cosanti Foundation
6433 Doubletree Road
Scottsdale, AZ 85253

Taliesin West
Scottsdale, AZ 85261

Building materials

Adobe Bricks
P.O. Box 969
San Juan Pueblo, NM 87566

Tiles de Santa Fe, Inc.
Route 5
Box 240
Santa Fe, NM 87501

Southwestern Furnishings

The Adobe Wall
61 Town and Country Village
Houston, TX 77024

Architectural Antiques, Ltd.
1125 Canyon Road
Santa Fe, NM 87501

Beyond Horizons
7050 East Third Avenue
Scottsdale, AZ 85251

Caldarella's Antiques
10167 Socorro Drive
El Paso, TX 79927

Country Cottage Antiques
247 E. Main Street
Fredericksburg, TX 78624

Dell Woodworks
401 Rodeo Road
Santa Fe, NM 87505

Dooling Woodworks
525 Airport Road
Santa Fe, NM 87501

Jackalope Pottery
2820 Cerrillos Road
Santa Fe, NM 87501

Jim Wagner Painted Furniture
P.O. Box 2110
Taos, NM 87571

McMillan's Woodworks
1326 Rufina Circle
Santa Fe, NM 87501

Que Pasa
7051 East Fifth Avenue
Scottsdale, AZ 85251

Rand & Co.
4 Newtown Lane
East Hampton, NY 11937

Reed Brothers
Turner Stations
Sebastopol, CA 95472

Richard Mulligan
8471 Melrose Avenue
Los Angeles, CA 90069

Santa Fe Interiors
214 Old Santa Fe Trail
Santa Fe, NM 87501

Sombraje
P.O. Box 295
Dixon, NM 87527

Southwest Spanish Craftsman
112 West San Francisco Street
Santa Fe, NM 87501

Sundance
R.R. 3
Box 624-C
Sundance, UT 84604

Taos Furniture
232 Galisteo Street
P.O. Box 2624
Santa Fe, NM 87504

Zona
484 Broome Street
New York, NY 10013

Gardens

Arboretum at Flagstaff
South Woody Mountain Road
Flagstaff, AZ 86002

Arizona-Sonora Desert Museum
2021 North Kinney Road
Tucson, AZ 85743

Boyce Thompson
Southwestern Arboretum
U.S. Highway 60
P.O. Box AB
Superior, AZ 85273

Desert Botanical Garden
1201 N. Galvin Parkway
Phoenix, AZ 85008

Living Desert State Park
U.S. Highway 285
Carlsbad, NM 88220

Native Seeds/SEARCH
2150 North Alvernon Way
Tucson, AZ 85712

Organ Pipe Cactus
National Monument
Route 1
Box 100
Ajo, AZ 85321

Pinnacle Peak Village Desert Garden
8711 East Pinnacle Peak
Scottsdale, AZ 85255

Saguaro National Monument
3693 South Old Spanish Trail
Tucson, AZ 85730

Tohono Chul Park
7366 North Paseo del Norte
Tucson, AZ 85704

Tucson Botanical Gardens
2150 North Alvernon Way
Tucson, AZ 85712

Food

Albuquerque Traders
P.O. Box 10170
Albuquerque, NM 87114
chiles and chile powder

Blue Heaven (Blue Corn Connection)
8812 4th Street N.W.
Alameda, NM 87114
blue cornmeal products

Casa Lucas Market
2934 24th Street
San Francisco, CA 94110
chiles

Casados Farms
Box 1269
San Juan Pueblo, NM 87566
chiles

Coyote Kitchens
102 West San Francisco Street, Suite 1
Sante Fe, NM 87501
wide range of
Southwestern specialities

Dean and Deluca
560 Broadway
New York, NY 10012
chiles, blue cornmeal

Flor del Rio Decorations
P.O. Box 6
Velarde, NM 87582
ristras

Jane Butel's Pecos Valley Spice Co.
142 Lincoln Avenue
Santa Fe, NM 87051
wide range of
Southwestern specialties

Josie's Best Tortilla Factory
1130 Agua Fria Street
P.O. Box 5525
Santa Fe, NM 87501
chiles; blue cornmeal products

Midwest Imports
1121 South Clinton
Chicago, IL 60607
chiles

Señor Murphy
La Fonda Hotel
Santa Fe, NM 87501
piñon candies

Notable Restaurants:

Baby Routh
2708 Routh Street
Dallas, TX 75201

Coyote Cafe
102 West San Francisco Street
Santa Fe, NM 87501

Janos
Tucson Museum of Art Plaza
150 N. Main Avenue
Tucson, AZ 85701

Routh Street Cafe
3005 Routh Street
Dallas, TX 75201

Saint Estephe
2460 N. Sepulveda Boulevard
Manhattan Beach, CA 90266

138

Crafts

Museum Collections

Albuquerque Museum
2000 Mountain Road Northwest
P.O. Box 1293
Albuquerque, NM 87103

Anasazi Heritage Center
27501 Highway 184
Dolores, CO 81323

The Arizona Museum
1002 W. Van Buren Street
Phoenix, AZ 85007

Bent Gallery and Museum
18 Bent Street
Taos, NM 87571

The Brooklyn Museum
Eastern Parkway
Brooklyn, NY 11238

Centennial Museum
University of Texas at El Paso
El Paso, TX 79902

Colorado River Indian Tribes Museum
Route 1, Box 23-B
Parker, AZ 85344

Deming Luna Mimbres Museum
301 South Silver
Deming, NM 88030

Denver Art Museum
100 West 14th Avenue
Denver, CO 80204

Denver Museum of Natural History
2001 Colorado Boulevard
Denver, CO 80207

El Paso Museum of History
12901 Gateway Boulevard West
El Paso, TX 79927

Field Museum
Roosevelt Road and Lake Shore Drive
Chicago, IL 60605

The Heard Museum
22 East Monte Vista Road
Phoenix, AZ 85004

Indian Pueblo Cultural Center
2401 12th Street Northwest
Albuquerque, NM 87104

Logan Museum of Anthropology
South Campus Circle
Beloit College
Beloit, WI 53511

Lost City Museum
Box 807
Overton, NV 89040

Millicent Rogers Museum
P.O. Box A
Taos, NM 87571

Museum of Anthropology
100 Swallow Hall
University of Missouri
Columbia, MO 65211

Museum of Indian Heritage
6040 De Long Road
Indianapolis, IN 46254

Museum of International Folk Art
706 Camino Lejo
P.O. Box 2087
Santa Fe, NM 87504

Museum of Northern Arizona
Route 4, Box 720
Flagstaff, AZ 86001

The Museum of the American Indian
Broadway and 155th Street
New York, NY 10032

Peabody Museum of Archaeology
and Ethnology
Harvard University
11 Divinity
Cambridge, MA 02138

Portland Art Museum
1219 S.W. Park
Portland, OR 97205

Southwest Museum
234 Museum Drive
P.O. Box 128
Los Angeles, CA 90042

Tantaquidgeon Indian Museum
1819 Norwich–New London Turnpike
Uncasville, CT 06382

Wheelwright Museum
of the American Indian
704 Camino Lejo
Santa Fe, NM 87504

William Hammond Mathers Museum
Indiana University
601 East Eighth Street
Bloomington, IN 47405

Wilson Museum
P.O. Box 196
Castine, ME 04421

Shops, Galleries, and Shows

Channing Dale Throckmorton
53 Old Santa Fe Trail
Santa Fe, NM 87501

Common Ground
19 Greenwich Avenue
New York, NY 10014

Crownpoint Navajo Rug Auction
Crownpoint, NM 87313

Davis Mather Folk Art Gallery
141 Lincoln Avenue
Santa Fe, NM 87501

Dewey Galleries, Ltd.
74 E. San Francisco Street
Santa Fe, NM 87501

Hopi Arts and Crafts
P.O. Box 37
Second Mesa, AZ 86043

Hubbell Trading Post
P.O. Box 388
Ganado, AZ 86505

Doodlet's Shop
120 Don Gaspar Avenue
Santa Fe, NM 87501

Economos Works of Art
225 Canyon Road
Santa Fe, NM 87501

Eight Northern Pueblos
Artist and Crafts Show
P.O. Box 969
San Juan Pueblo, NM 87566
held for 2 days each July

El Rincón
Kit Carson Street
Taos, NM 87571

Four Winds Gallery
1167 3rd Street South
Olde Naples, FL 33940

Gallery 10 Inc.
7045 3rd Avenue
Scottsdale, AZ 85251

Garland's Navajo Rugs
Highway 179
Post Office Box 851
Sedona, AZ 86336

The Hand and the Spirit Gallery
4222 North Marshall Way
Scottsdale, AZ 85251

Hurst Gallery
53 Mount Aubum Street
Cambridge, MA 02138

Indian Craft Shop
1801 C Street
Department of Interior
Washington, DC 20240

Indian Market
P.O. Box 1964
Santa Fe, NM 87501
held annually
the third weekend in August

Keams Canyon Arts & Crafts
P.O. Box 607, Highway 264
Keams Canyon, AZ 86034

Lee's Indian Crafts
1833 East Indian School Road
Phoenix, AZ 85016

American Renaissance
1 Old Durango Road
P.O. Box 1570
Pagosa Springs, CO 81147

The Medicine Wheel Gallery
2234 North Fremont Street
Chicago, IL 60614

Morning Star Gallery
513 Canyon Road
Santa Fe, NM 87501

The Native American Art Gallery
215 Windward Avenue
Venice, CA 90291

Native American
Artifacts and Antiquities
125 East Palace Avenue
Santa Fe, NM 87501

Native American Cooperative
Box 301
San Carlos Apache Reservation
San Carlos, AZ 85550

The Rainbow Man
107 East Palace Avenue
Santa Fe, NM 87501

Shepler Gallery
103 Bear Creek Avenue
P.O. Box 374
Morrison, CO 80465

Thunderbird Shop
40 West Broadway
Tucson, AZ 85701

Tom Bahti Indian Arts
450 West Paseo Redondo
Tucson, AZ 85701

Tony Reyna's Shops
Taos, NM 87571

Bibliography

Abbey, Edward. *Desert Solitaire: A Season in the Wilderness.* New York: Touchstone/Simon and Schuster, 1968.

Andrews, Jean. *Peppers: The Domesticated Capsicums.* Austin, Tex.: University of Texas Press, 1984.

Apa Productions, eds. *American Southwest.* Singapore: Apa Publications/Insight Guides, 1988.

Austin, Mary. *The Land of Journeys' Ending.* Tucson, Ariz.: University of Arizona Press, 1924/1983.

Bahti, Mark. *Pueblo Stories and Storytellers.* Tucson, Ariz.: Treasure Chest Publications, Inc., 1988.

Bodine, John J. *Taos Pueblo: A Walk through Time.* Santa Fe, N.M.: Lightning Tree, 1977.

Boyd, E. *Popular Arts of Spanish New Mexico.* Santa Fe, N.M.: Museum of New Mexico Press, 1974.

Brierly, Cornelia. *Desert Life: Desert Foliage at Taliesin West.* Scottsdale, Ariz.: Frank Lloyd Wright Foundation, 1988.

Bromberg, Erik, *The Hopi Approach to the Art of Kachina Doll Carving.* West Chester, Pa.: Schiffer Publishing Ltd. 1986.

Brown, Ellen. *Southwest Tastes.* Tucson, Ariz.: HP Books, 1987.

Burba, Nora, and Paula Panich. *The Desert Southwest.* New York: Bantam Books, 1987.

Cameron, Sheila MacNiven, and the Staff of *New Mexico Magazine. New Mexico Magazine's More of the Best from New Mexico Kitchens.* Santa Fe, N.M.: New Mexico Magazine, 1983.

Chronic, Halka. *Pages of Stone: Geology of Western National Parks & Monuments; 3: The Desert Southwest.* Seattle: The Mountaineers, 1986.

Dent, Huntley. *The Feast of Santa Fe: Cooking of the American Southwest.* New York: Simon and Schuster, 1985.

Desert Botanical Garden Staff. *Arizona Highways Presents Desert Wildflowers.* Phoenix, Ariz.: Arizona Department of Transportation, 1988.

Desert Botanical Garden Staff. *Plants and People of the Sonoran Desert: Trail Guide.* Phoenix, Ariz.: Desert Botanical Garden. n.d.

Douglas, Jim. *The Complete New Mexico Cookbook.* Santa Fe, N.M.: Elena's Kitchen, 1977.

Ensrud, Barbara. *American Vineyards.* New York. Stuart, Tebori & Chang, Inc. 1988.

Glassie, Henry. *The Spirit of Folk Art: The Girard Collection at the Museum of International Folk Art.* New York: Harry N. Abrams, Inc.; Santa Fe, N.M.: Museum of New Mexico Press, 1989.

Greer, Anne Lindsay. *Foods of the Sun: Cooking of the West and Southwest.* New York: Harper & Row, 1988.

Haselton, Scott E. *Cactus & Succulents and How to Grow Them.* Phoenix, Ariz.: Desert Botanical Garden. n.d.

Hodge, Carle. *Ruins Along the River.* Tucson, Ariz.: Southwest Parks and Monuments Association, 1986.

International Folk Art Foundation. *Multiple Visions: A Common Bond, The Girard Foundation Collection.* Santa Fe, N.M.: Museum of New Mexico Press, 1982.

Kirk, Ruth. *An Inside Look at the Arizona-Sonora Desert Museum.* Tucson, Ariz.: Arizona-Sonora Desert Museum, 1989.

Landau, Carl, and Katie Landau with Kathy Kincade. *Festivals of the Southwest.* San Francisco: Landau Communications, 1989.

Lisle, Laurie. *Portrait of an Artist: A Biography of Georgia O'Keeffe.* New York: Washington Square Press/Pocket Books, 1980.

Marshall, Ann E., and Mary H. Brennan. *The Heard Museum: History and Collections.* Phoenix, Ariz.: The Heard Museum, 1989.

Mather, Christine, and Sharon Woods. *Santa Fe Style.* New York: Rizzoli, 1986.

Maxwell Museum of Anthropology. *Seven Families in Pueblo Pottery.* Albuquerque, N.M.: University of New Mexico Press, 1974.

Mays, Buddy. *Indian Villages of the Southwest.* San Francisco: Chronicle Books, 1985.

Miller, Mark Charles. *Coyote Cafe: Foods from the Great Southwest.* Berkeley, Calif.: Ten Speed Press, 1989.

Ortiz, Alfonso, ed. *Handbook of North American Indians, Volumes 9/10: Southwest.* Washington, D.C.: Smithsonian Institution, 1979/1983.

Pfeiffer, Bruce Brooks, and Gerald Nordland, eds. *Frank Lloyd Wright In the Realm of Ideas.* Carbondale and Edwardsville, Ill.: Southern Illinois University Press, 1988.

Phillips, Judith. *Southwestern Landscaping with Native Plants.* Santa Fe, N.M.: Museum of New Mexico Press, 1987.

Rodee, Marian. *Weaving of the Southwest.* West Chester, Pa.: Schiffer Publishing, Ltd., 1987.

Russell, Marian Sloane. *Land of Enchantment: Memoirs of Marian Russell Along the Santa Fe Trail,* as dictated to Mrs. Hall Russell, ed. Albuquerque, N.M.: 1981, reprint.

Sedlar, John, with Norman Kolpas. *Modern Southwest Cuisine.* New York: Simon and Schuster, 1986.

The Sierra Club Guides to the National Parks of the Desert Southwest. New York: Steward, Tabori & Chang, 1984.

Smith, Deborahann. *Arizona Cactus: A Guide to Unique Varieties.* Frederick, Colo.: Renaissance House, 1988.

Soleri, Paolo. *Arcosanti: An Urban Laboratory?* Santa Monica, Calif.: VTI Press, 1987.

Spears, Beverley. *American Adobes.* Albuquerque, N.M.: University of New Mexico Press, 1986.

Storrer, William Allin. *The Architecture of Frank Lloyd Wright.* Cambridge, Mass.: MIT Press, 1974.

Taylor, Ann, with Lila DeWindt. *Southwestern Ornamentation & Design: The Architecture of John Gaw Meem.* Santa Fe, N.M.: Sunstone Press, 1989.

Taylor, Lonn, and Dessa Bokides. *New Mexican Furniture, 1600–1940.* Santa Fe, N.M.: Museum of New Mexico Press, 1987.

Toulouse, Betty, *Pueblo Pottery of the New Mexico Indians.* Santa Fe, N.M.: Museum of New Mexico Press, 1977.

Warren, Nancy Hunter. *New Mexico Style: A Source Book of Traditional Architectural Details.* Santa Fe, N.M.: Museum of New Mexico Press, 1986.

———. *Villages of Hispanic New Mexico.* Santa Fe, N.M.: School of American Research Press, 1987.

Weigle, Marta, and Peter White. *The Lore of New Mexico.* Albuquerque, N.M.: University of New Mexico Press, 1988.

Whiteford, Andrew Hunter, Steward Peckham, Rick Dillingham, Nancy Fox, and Kate Peck Kent. *I Am Here: Two Thousand Years of Southwest Indian Arts and Culture.* Santa Fe, N.M.: Museum of New Mexico Press, 1989.

Wilder, Janos. *Janos: Recipes & Tales from a Southwest Restaurant.* Berkeley, Calif.: Ten Speed Press, 1989.

Wright, Barton. *Hopi Kachinas: The Complete Guide to Collecting Kachina Dolls.* Flagstaff, Ariz.: Northland Publishing, 1977.

Wright, Frank Lloyd. *A Testament.* New York: Horizon Press, 1957.

144